The Ray Wood Story:

Confessions of a Black NYPD Cop in the Assassination of Malcolm X

AS TOLD TO REGGIE WOOD
COAUTHORED BY LIZZETTE SALADO

ISBN: 978-1-7366027-0-6

Library of Congress Control Number: 1-10121603551

Author: Reginald E Wood, Jr.

Coauthor: Lizzette Salado

Cover Designer: Rude Bwoy Graphics & Printing
https://www.rudebwoygraphics.com/

Copyeditor: Alan Roberts
www.alanroberts.nyc

Photo Contributor: Angela G. Wood

Research Contributors: L.E.J Rachell (Head of the CORE Legacy Project corenyc.org), Susan Brownmiller, Breonna Nicole Wood

www.theraywoodstory.com

Published by Madera Enterprises

First Printing Edition 2021

In Loving Memory

Raymond A. Wood, 1933-2020.

This short memoir is based on Ray Wood's account of his past, shared verbally with me over the course of many in-depth conversations. Ray was explicit in detail, knowingly and clearly asking me to keep a record of his account for the purpose of sharing his confession with the public after his passing. This account is reaffirmed by Ray in his signed confession letter that he left with me. Various articles and papers that discuss Ray, especially in relation to the speculation that surrounded him regarding the Malcolm X assassination, have been referenced throughout the book and are referenced in the bibliography. Other narrative detail, such as dialogue, has been added to help convey Ray's story to the reader.

Table of Contents

Foreword

By Chenjerai Kumanyika, PhD
Assistant Professor, Rutgers University
Son of Makaza Kumanyika (Herb Callender)

When I learned that Ray Wood, a former Black NYPD agent provocateur, had shared his life story, I wasn't sure how to respond. On the orders of the NYPD's Bureau of Special Services and Investigation (BOSSI), Wood infiltrated numerous Black political organizations during the mid to late 1960's. He was recruited specifically to embed himself in their work, surveil them, provoke them into acts of property destruction and violence, entrap them and then testify against them. His first arrest was my father, Herbert Callender, leader of the Bronx chapter of Congress of Racial Equality (CORE). No matter how informed one might be about the ongoing, state-sanctioned violence of police, red squads, or the FBI, this kind of story can and should allow us to feel the rage anew.

Although I felt that Wood's family made a courageous and correct choice to write and share his memoir, I wasn't sure if I could muster the emotional endurance to take in the account you're about to read. Ray Wood had the privilege of living a long life with the freedom to tell his story, never having faced accountability. Why should he now be allowed to present himself as a whole person, when his actions helped reduce people we loved, and who loved justice, to violent caricatures?

As painful and infuriating as it might be to look through Ray Wood's eyes, I feel his perspective carries essential lessons for those of us who seek to dismantle oppressive systems at their roots. The most important of these lessons from Wood's story extend powerfully into the present, offering us essential guidance in the ongoing fight for justice.

First, though Ray Wood bears responsibility for his actions, he was not their ultimate author. His memoir allows us to look more fully at the root of the poisonous tree and see a Black man, born into circumstances he didn't control, who ultimately became a cog in the vast architecture of the repressive U.S. policing apparatus. You will never hear me debate anyone calling Ray Wood "Judas," but we should use this metaphor with caution. The illusion that one's ethnicity can be conflated with their political commitment is precisely what allowed Wood to gain entry to so many organizations, so easily. There are obvious lessons here for the 690,000+ officers in the United States today, but not only for them. Despite the efforts of COINTELPRO, Red Squads and agent provocateurs, the victories of the civil rights movement enabled a new wave of Black elites to enter the managerial classes. This meant a change in fortune for their strata, but also placed them as managers in the military, corporations, universities, local government, and the full spectrum of institutions that reproduce and manage black suffering. Therefore, rather than stopping at the label of Judas, it may be more instructive for us to reflect on what his story teaches each of us about navigating our own employers and business partners, and coming to grips with their impact on the lives of Black people and other vulnerable folks.

Let us be clear. Led by J. Edgar Hoover, the FBI and NYPD assigned Ray Wood and other agent provocateurs to infiltrate organizations that were fighting against violence. Those movements were fighting against the violence of systematic racist and capitalist oppression. By Wood's own admission, organizers like Malcolm X, my father, and many others were targeted, entrapped, arrested, and attacked for protesting racist hiring practices, segregation, voter suppression, housing practices and the organized violence of police and prisons.

Why then is the state (NYPD, FBI, etc.) so invested in presenting these organizations as violent? The details of Ray Wood's recruitment teach us that state-sponsored provocateur-ism was a response to a shift in the movement toward more strategic, effective, and militant non-violent action by a spectrum of Black organizations. Whatever their flaws, groups such as Malcom X's Organization of African-American Unity (OAAU), CORE, Revolutionary Action Movement (RAM), and the Black Panthers were building powerful domestic and international networks with actions and rhetorical appeals amplifying the systematic racial terror of the United States and making the terms of struggle increasingly clear.

In the face of this justified resistance, then and now, the NYPD, FBI, and other apparatuses of U.S. empire have no ethical, moral, or even constitutional counter argument. Instead, characterizing these movements as violent is an attempt to distract attention from the conditions these organizations were protesting in order to delegitimize them. Only months before the recruitment of Ray Wood, the NYPD strung up and brutally beat Jesse Roberts – a Black auto mechanic who reported a stolen car. My father was among the organizers who handcuffed themselves inside the headquarters of police commissioner Michael J. Murphy, demanding justice. Instead of addressing the savage beating of an innocent person, or any person for that matter, police commissioner Murphy responded by claiming he must protect the city against "extremist violence." He later clarified he was speaking specifically of Malcom X, Jesse Gray, and my father, Herb Callender.

Ray Wood should not have been surprised to find that the labelling of Black freedom movements as dangerous and violent set the stage for their violent oppression. The blood images of what his work unleashed haunted him until his death. Today, labels like the FBI's Black Identity Extremists reactivate a vast reservoir of centuries of racist representations casting the entire black diaspora as irrationally violent. In the U.S., the modern institution of policing was

forged partially from vast slave patrols criminalizing the entire Black population.

Centuries later, the powerful lines of continuity between the repressive function of policing during the civil rights movement, and during our present struggles, should be at the forefront of national and international conversations. It would be absurd to imagine these wounds have healed; they are still being inflicted on contemporary organizers.

Clarity on these matters is especially urgent at a time when progressive elected officials insist on describing the problem of police as one of "mistrust" between police and Black communities, and "broken systems" that can be remedied with piecemeal reforms. The tremendous resources and planning from multiple tiers of U.S. government behind Ray Wood lay waste to this mythology, revealing a system that is working according to its design. Centuries of reform have made this system more vast and more lethal, and the radical work of dismantling it is a step toward moving forward, healing, and building the safe communities we all desire.

-Chenjerai Kumanyika, son of Makaza Kumanyika (Herb Callender)

"I'm for truth, no matter who tells it. I'm for justice, no matter who it's for or against."

-Malcolm X

Prologue

November 25, 2020

As the grease heats in preparation for the turkey that is about to be fried to crisp perfection, the remaining Thanksgiving Day preparations have the rest of the house in a flurry. While the children play in the yard and various side dishes are being prepared in the kitchen, I find myself putting the finishing touches on the turkey when my cell phone rings.

"Hey Dad, what's going on?" I answer with the impatient tone typically reserved for a phone call that just halted the frying of food.

"I have some rough news, son. Cousin Ray passed away last night."

This was the call that I'd been both expecting and fearing. My cousin, Raymond A. Wood, had a secret that had loomed over him most of his adult life and kept him essentially isolated from society; a secret that has now become my responsibility to share with the world. It is my duty to tell Ray's story not only as his entrusted confidante, but also as a Black man, to ensure history is set straight and the world knows what truly happened in the mid-1960s.

Part
One

December 2010

My introduction to cousin Ray began in early December of 2010. I received a phone call from my father Reginald Wood Sr., a retired US Sergeant Major with a no-nonsense attitude. After our usual brief greeting, my father began telling me about our almost 80-year-old cousin, Raymond A. Wood. Immediately, the name resonated with me and brought back a news story I remembered from many years ago. I had heard the name before; there was a story from back in the 1960's about the Statue of Liberty and a foiled bombing attack, but I was unsure if this was the same guy. No one in the family had seen or heard from Ray since that period, which further piqued my curiosity about this man. According to family word of mouth, he'd lived in near obscurity since the 1960's and had very limited interaction with society since then.

The Sergeant Major rarely calls to engage in small talk or to speak about other family members. Because of this unusual start to the conversation, I was immediately intrigued and knew there had to be a specific reason for this call. My father explained that Ray had recently reached out to him and wanted to reconnect with the family.

“Reggie, our cousin Ray has had a tough time of it, and I’m surprised he reached out to me after all these years of silence,” my father explained. “I have a feeling he needs his family right now.”

“Ray, the cousin that you grew up with?” I asked. My father had mentioned Ray to me in the past, whenever he spoke about his childhood and teenage years, but I’d never met him face-to-face.

“Yup, that’s the one,” my dad chuckled and then fell silent for a moment. “We had some good times growin’ up.”

By the end of the conversation, it was clear that reuniting with cousin Ray meant a lot to the family and to Ray himself. I was tasked with extending him an invitation to visit our family, with the hopes that this reunion would lead to Ray’s transition to the Tampa Bay area, where we lived. We all thought it'd be nice for him to live near me and my family. Ray was a beloved member of our extended family and his reclusion had caused strife and concern for many, so this recent decision of his to break his isolation was a cause for celebration.

It was settled. I was going to reach out to Ray and hopefully bring him back to the family.

Before connecting with Ray, I admit I was a little apprehensive about how the meeting would go. *Would he like me? Would I like him? What should I expect from an almost recluse, older, distant cousin?* Packing those questions away, I shouldered on with the task at hand and reached out to Ray. He had been expecting my call and shortly into the conversation we scheduled a time for him to come out and visit. I booked him a flight from North Carolina to Florida and arranged to pick him up from the airport, so that I could take him out to lunch. I wanted to get to know him over a meal while speaking with him one-on-one.

I arrived at the Tampa International Airport fifteen minutes prior to Ray's arrival time. As I drove around the airport several times waiting for Ray to appear at the doors, I ruminated on where I should take him to lunch. The Tampa Bay area overflows with all sorts of delicious cuisine including authentic Mexican food trucks, Cuban fare, and traditional American dining. I settled on one of my usual favorites, a bar and grill restaurant near my home that overlooks the water. With a broad range of seafood and drinks packing a punch for a reasonable price, I always enjoy my meals there.

As I made my fourth loop around the airport, I received the call from Ray letting me know that he had his luggage and was heading towards the exit. Two minutes later I pulled up to the curb alongside Ray and got out to greet him. "Ray! I'm glad you came to visit us," I gave him a quick hug and reached for his luggage to load it into the trunk. "How was your flight?"

"It's alright, I got it," Ray said nonchalantly, heaving his suitcase into the back. "And my flight wasn't too bad. I'm just glad it was a short trip. These old legs were starting to cramp up on me." Even at his age, Ray was a relatively tall guy, just over six feet, so I could imagine that small airplane seats could get quite uncomfortable.

"Well, soon we'll be having a nice meal and some drinks," I told Ray as we drove away from the airport. "I hope you like the beach and liquor," I joked.

"One of the main reasons I'm here!" Ray laughed jovially, nudging me lightly with his elbow.

We chatted most of the ride to the restaurant and continued our comfortable conversation throughout our meal, keeping topics light and just really getting to know each other. Despite the original wariness I felt about meeting Ray for the first time, I soon gained insight into the mind of a quiet, resilient man with a presence that emanated history and a sort of wisdom that can only come from experience. I could tell Ray was a character with many quirks, but I could also sense that he was earnest in his desire to reconnect with us. Despite his peculiar personality, I knew my family would welcome him with open arms. I'd already described to them Ray's significance to my father's family and we were all onboard with giving an older man the chance to feel part of a community again.

We spent a few days with Ray, getting to know each other and relating tales about our family on that side. One of our first trips out with the entire family was to one of Florida's well-known scenic beaches. We spent the day enjoying the sunshine, warm breezes, and the soft sand of Anna-Maria Island. As the kids ran on the beach throwing footballs and attempting cartwheels, the adults laid under umbrellas sipping drinks and talking with each other. As I walked over to the cooler to grab myself a bottle of water to cool off from the blazing Florida sun, I glanced over to see Ray laughing loudly at a joke someone had just told. I could tell he was really enjoying himself and having a great time with everyone. It was deeply satisfying to see him getting comfortable with us and settling in, and I could easily imagine Ray becoming a central part of the Wood family dynamic.

(Ray Wood during a family trip to the beach, 2011. Photo by Angela G. Wood)

I think our beautiful beaches are one of the things that convinced Ray to ultimately decide to move to Florida. I started taking him around to different areas of Florida near our home, hoping we'd find an area he could envision himself living in and would like to rent out.

I'd only known Ray a short time, but I still shouldn't have been surprised that he already had a plan in mind for what he wanted. It was only a few days into the trip when we found Ray a home in an area he enjoyed and was close to my family. The lease was signed, and Ray would be a Florida resident by mid-February. His reintegration into the family fold was official. I arranged a flight to North Carolina so I could help him pack, and then the two of us would drive to Florida together.

This arrangement ultimately provided the opportunity to really get to know and understand Ray on an even deeper level. I believe it was a combination of the natural kinship that comfortably existed between us, along with his desire to connect with another human, that led him to share his life story with me over the course of this car road trip and through other conversations that would take place over the years. During the 10-hour drive from North Carolina to Florida, Ray described what his life was like as a young boy growing up during the 1940's and 1950's, as well as his short experience living with his mother Helen and father Adolphis Wood, a merchant seaman marine by trade. Ray had lived a turbulent early childhood, starting with being left at an orphanage by his mother at a young age.

I was shocked when Ray told me this. Reminiscing on this part of Ray's story, I imagine this was not something anyone in the family was proud of nor wanted to remember, which is probably why I was unaware of it until then.

Shortly after being orphaned, Ray's aunt Annie B (who is also my grandmother, on my father's side) went to the orphanage to claim custody of Ray, after being told by Adolphis that Ray had been left there a few months prior. When my grandmother picked Ray up from the orphanage, he stayed with her in New York for a couple of years until he was able to go live with the extended family in South Carolina. Aunt Easter, Annie B's aunt, and her husband William Henry Lilly lived in Chester, South Carolina and were well known for taking in youths needing a home. But they were unable to take Ray in while he was still a very small child, so when Ray was old enough, he moved to South Carolina and lived with the Lilly's. Easter and William Lilly did their best to care for him, ensuring that he didn't end up in the system, outside of the care of our family.

It was during this time in Ray's life that he formed a close bond with my father. Reginald Sr. was four years younger than Ray and had also moved from New York to South Carolina, only a few years following Ray. By the time that Reginald Sr. moved to South Carolina, Ray had already lived there for a couple of years and was somewhat acclimated to the differences between the south and New York. In the 1950's, Jim Crow laws and extreme racial segregation was even more evident in the south than the north. Both young teen boys went from living in New York, where a Black person had slightly more liberties and freedom from persecution than those living in post-Confederate states, to living in South Carolina, a state riddled with overt racism and bias.

When Ray arrived at this part in the retelling of his youth, he became very animated and was excited to share some of the childhood experiences they had lived together. Ray and my father became as close as brothers during their time in South Carolina, and like with most teenage siblings turned adults, stories of their rowdiness and youthful escapades tend to be told with a wistfully nostalgic, faraway look in the eye.

"Me and your father together as youngin's, boy did we raise some hell!" Ray exclaimed. "Aunt Easter and Uncle Henry sure did have their hands full, especially when Ernie first moved down. Ya' know we used to call him by his middle name back then?"

"Yup. Ernest, same as me," I told him.

“Well, when Ernie first moved to South Carolina we got ourselves into a bit of trouble here and there,” Ray said.

“Doesn’t surprise me,” I laughed, thinking about how Ray and my father acted around each other as grown men. They were a riot, always joking and teasing each other. “I can imagine y’all just tearing up the town.”

Ray chuckled. “Not quite. We actually spent six months stuck working for some White man when we got into trouble for chopping some trees down. Ernie and I had seen a guy on the side of the road with a large peach basket carrying some chopped wood. When we asked him what he was doing, he said he was selling it. And as young boys we thought ‘Great idea!’

“So, we went to a field right across the house and took one of Uncle Henry's axes and started chopping down trees, thinking we were slick and were going to make some quick cash off this. We were barely one tree down when a large white man came runnin’ up to us, face red yelling ‘Boy! What in the damn hell are you doing?’

“Thinking nothing of it, I told him, ‘Selling some wood, want some?’ When I said this, Ernie snorted into his hand. I turned around and gave him a dirty look. When the White man asked, ‘Whose boy is you?’ I said, ‘We’re Bud Lilly’s boys.’ Now, mind you, Bud Lilly

(Uncle Henry) was a mulatto. One of his parents were White and he was real light skinned, so the White folks back then tended to give him a little bit more respect than other Black people.

"When the man brought back the sheriff and told him that we were trespassing, we were only made to work on this White man's land for six months instead of taking us into the town jail. We were Bud Lilly's boys."

I scoffed, "What about the guy you saw with the basket selling wood?"

"Oh, he was still there on the side of the road. Stayed there selling that wood for weeks while we worked on this man's land for chopping one tree," Ray said. "But he was White, and we were young Black boys. That's just the way things went."

(Photo of Reginald Wood Sr. (aka, Ernie). Circa mid 1940's)

As we continued on with the drive, Ray told me another anecdote of him and my dad in South Carolina, this one also occurring when my father was freshly arrived from New York. Our family has a longstanding belief that life insurance is crucially important, and the Lilly's steadfastly followed this family rule. Back then, the insurance collector would let himself into the Lilly residence once a month to collect the insurance payment waiting for him inside the door.

"Well, the first time the insurance man came by the house after your dad had moved in, there was a huge showdown," Ray said. "Ernie thought this White man was breaking in! He picked up the fireplace poker that was nearby and started beating the man with the stick. I overheard the commotion in the living room and ran straight there. I was about to get Ernie to stop when my Aunt Easter came in the room. She said, 'What in the damn hell are you doing?'

"Aunt Easter grabbed the broom and beat the shit outta Ernie. Man, when I tell you she opened up a can of whoop ass."

"Well, damn," I said to Ray. "I might start beating someone that comes into my house like that, too. How was he supposed to know?"

"Like father like son," Ray laughed softly. "That's exactly what your dad said at the time. And Aunt Easter told him that that doesn't matter. That White man was KKK. She said, 'This ain't New York. You embarrassed that man! All we need is the white hoods to come knockin' on our door. You best learn quick that the White people here are NOT to be messed with. You hear?'"

"Holy shit! What did the guy say?" I asked him. I couldn't believe that my dad had had this experience with a KKK member!

"Aunt Easter was just apologizing over and over, telling him that Ernie didn't know any better, he had just got here from New York. The man yelled, 'Well he better learn before we teach him a lesson!" and stormed off. Uncle Bill spent the next three sleepless nights by our front door, with a rifle in hand in case the white hoods and torches came for us in the dark. We were lucky they never came. I think Aunt Easter's ass whooping helped."

In the years following these two incidents, Ray went on to become a high school football star with a strong throwing arm. He excelled at the sport and had potential to take his game to another level, perhaps even play professionally. However, when Ray was an older teenager his family was struck by a terrible accident that changed his life's trajectory. His father, Adolphis Wood, was a strong, muscular man who worked on large ships as a United States Merchant Marine. When Ray was in his final year of high school, Adolphis was killed in a devastating accident onboard a ship while overseas. Upset by what had happened and ready to leave home, Ray left school and eventually joined the US Air Force a few years later.

(Adolphis Wood, Circa 1940's.)

While on that long car ride home, Ray also described his career as an undercover New York Police Department detective; he told me about what it was like working as a Black officer in the 60's and 70s, when many of his coworkers were men that looked down on people of color. He shared several anecdotes of his time in New York, including the threats, insults, and discrimination that he constantly faced, both in and out of uniform.

"You know, it wasn't unusual to have a White man call you by some slur or to have a White woman sneer at you. But the sting would always still be there," Ray explained. "I got some of the worst of it from the Irish policemen in the NYPD. You'd think that immigrants not from the US would feel like an outsider, too. But it was as if they tried even harder to make themselves belong."

"Yeah, I can see that," I replied. "Even now things are still like that, like with Black officers who are harder on Black people so they can try to fit in and not be accused of playing favorites. Even some Latinos that against immigration. It just doesn't seem like it'd make any sense."

"Exactly. Some of those cats would beat up Black guys on the street for just jaywalking," Ray paused, taking a long sip of his water. "They weren't much better to us even when we were officers, too. They just saw Black cops as people playing a role that didn't belong to them. When I was an NYPD detective, there weren't many other Black cops over there. Hell, they just got their first Black officer only 50 years before me. And Jim Crow laws had barely just ended so the entire country seemed to be caught in limbo between change and the past. It was hard at times trying to feel like a part of the brotherhood."

As I listened to Ray tell me about his past experiences, I was appalled and yet sadly unsurprised to hear about the discrimination and oppression that he'd experienced in his youth.

February 2011

Ray was in his late 70's, but his keen eyes oozed intelligence and observed every detail of his surroundings. It soon became apparent there was a reason or behavior pattern to everything that he did or said. If a plan or outing was changed at the last minute, he questioned why and hesitated to participate. Ray never sat with his back to a window or door, always wanting to spot when someone initially entered the room.

One of the first things that he insisted on doing when he moved to Florida was to transfer his permit to carry a gun. "Reggie, I'm going into town tomorrow to get my gun permit," Ray announced one night over dinner. "I can't keep driving 'round here without my .38 on me. I ain't no sucka."

I began explaining to Ray that it was a long process to obtain a license to carry in Florida, and at his age he may not be given the permit. I didn't want him to become upset if they denied him and thought preparing him for rejection was a needed precaution. To my surprise, and slight dismay, Ray drove back home a few hours later and presented me with some paperwork and a signed permit.

"I told ya, Jack." he said to me, with a slightly crooked smile.

I asked myself, W*hy in hell would anyone give a concealed-carry gun permit to this 80-year-old man who's randomly narcoleptic, has shaking hands, and walks as if he's too proud to use a much-needed cane or walker?*

At this point I'd already heard many stories about Ray being a New York City hero cop back in the sixties. The work he'd done during that time caused him to move around judiciously the last few decades, fearing his career was going to come back to haunt him. This was actually the reason why Ray had spent so many years isolated from the family. I knew that he'd been a big shot undercover detective. We even used to jokingly call him "Cousin Snitch," teasing him about all of the undercover work he'd done. But still, that was all a very, very long time ago and I thought to myself, whoever was signing those gun permits should've screened him a little harder.

June 2011

The following year was filled with the usual events that make up our family's social life; birthdays, graduations, Sunday dinners, and holiday meals filled the calendar. And Ray was there for each one. He grew more comfortable with the family and soon a strong bond was formed. He was now an integral part of the family, a respected elder who always had an anecdote or some snippet of wisdom to share.

What we didn't yet realize was that those moments would be short lived. By mid-2011, Ray had received the news that his colon cancer was back and this time it had metastasized. This information devastated Ray; he had started his battle with colon cancer when he was first diagnosed with the disease in 1989 and the fight was over. He'd now been in remission for many years. Understandably, this news and the resulting cancer treatment led Ray to retreat into himself. For a while he stopped joining the family during our myriad of events, staying at home to deal with his disease in private.

A few weeks after his cancer diagnosis, on a non-descript evening when I was tucked into my home office sorting and paying bills, I received a call from Ray. Ever since his diagnosis he'd closed himself back up to the rest of the world and I was usually the one calling him, so I was a bit surprised to see his name on the caller i.d. The conversation was short and to the point. Ray asked me to come to his apartment for dinner, telling me that he had something important to talk about.

"But what's it about Ray?" I asked him, trying to get more details. "Is everything all right?"

"C'mon now," he scoffed, as if he wasn't the one calling me with a cryptic request out of the blue. "Just tell me what day works for you and I'll make sure to have some steaks on the grill."

Unsure what to expect, I made my way over to his apartment the following evening with a six pack in hand. Had I known the content of the conversation waiting for me at Ray's apartment, I would have brought Scotch instead. Arriving at his place, I immediately sensed his solemn demeanor and pensive silence. I tried to alleviate the mood with one of Ray's own usual phrases, "What's crackin', Jack?"

"Sit down, Reg. I need to tell you something and I don't want to take this shit to my grave."

What he told me that night has been a constant weight on my shoulders ever since. Ray's confession was given to me under the assumption that since his cancer was back, he wouldn't have much time left on this earth. Ray thought the end was near, and he was adamant that his secret would not die with him. At that point he'd lived in fear for 46 years, terrified that what he'd witnessed and participated in all those years ago would one day come back to haunt him. Ray made me promise him that night that I would share his account with the world only after he passed away, when he could no longer be punished or threatened.

After the night that Ray confessed to me, he managed to fight back against the cancer and got the chance to live for another nine years. With Ray having regained his health, the secret was pushed back down in fear of what might happen if it got out while he was alive. For these last nine years I have had to bear the burden of Ray's secret.

I am here now to tell Ray's story.

Part Two

1958

After completing four years in the Air Force, Ray was honorably discharged. He arrived in New York City with the usual bright eyes and ambition accompanying a 25-year-old man eager to experience all the world has to offer. Ray had spent the last few years in the military with his eyes set on the Big Apple, excited to take in the bright lights, the constant moving flow of crowds, the skyscrapers, celebrities… Ray could've gone on forever about New York City.

At 6'2 with olive brown skin and a shiny black afro, Ray was ready to take New York by force and was aching to experience the illustrious appeal of the big city. With his naturally athletic build and intelligent demeanor, he was the perfect candidate to fully experience all that the city had to offer, during both the day and night. He celebrated the luminous city at night, exploring restaurants such as *Frank's Restaurant* and *The Rooster.* Handsome and charming, he considered himself somewhat of a ladies' man and he enjoyed going out on the town, meeting women and wooing them with his words. During his old age, Ray would later find himself reminiscing on the scruples of his youth and reliving those nights filled with laughter, dancing, drinking, and all-around merriment.

During the day he found himself trying out different jobs to see what suited him the most, hoping to find his rightful place in the Big Apple. His employers during those years included a paper company, Chase Manhattan Bank, and a few gas and oil companies. Ray even found himself briefly enrolled at NYU and City College, before failing grades caused him to be disenrolled after just one semester.

Admittedly, Ray spent his first few years in New York making the most out of his youth in whichever way he pleased, occasionally focusing more on entertainment than work. While jumping around to different meaningless day jobs, Ray would spend his extracurricular time doing the typical things other young men did during the early 1960's. He went to the bars, danced with women, smoked a little bit of weed, and drank Scotch with his new friends. Those few years were spent living his life freely and letting the youthful vigor of the city envelop him. Eventually, Ray started giving more serious thought to his future and debated what he thought he could offer New York.

Amidst his work and his play, Ray also witnessed the civil rights movement that was sweeping the nation. In the summer of 1963, Ray was flirting with a young lady who was an active participant in the civil rights movement. In an attempt to impress and woo the woman, Ray joined her one day to go see some speakers in Harlem. The area was packed, with hundreds of Black people congregating to hear the much-awaited speaker that day, Malcolm X. Ray wasn't particularly interested in what the speech was about, but he couldn't help but be captivated by the speaker's voice. Malcolm X spoke with such passion, such command that Ray almost forgot for a moment why he was there. But only for a moment. The pretty girl Ray was with kept his mind occupied for most of that trip.

While Ray didn't yet understand the ideology or the passion that drove the protestors that day, he saw the madness that protests could bring to the city, both from the participants and the police. His experiences those first few years in New York ultimately combined to sculpt Ray's belief that he had a different purpose in life; his time in NYC showed him firsthand that the police department was severely lacking in diversity and representation. He believed he could make NYC a better place for the Black community by joining the police force and giving Black minorities an ally who could make a difference within the system.

He' d finally discovered what his path would be: the NYPD.

April 17, 1964

In early 1964 Ray filed an application with the New York Police Department with the hopes he'd be New York's finest police officer out patrolling the streets, stopping crime and catching the bad guys. Weeks of silence passed with not even a letter informing him of whether the position had been filled, if review was still pending, anything. Ray told me he started wondering if maybe he wasn't qualified enough or experienced enough, or if maybe he just wasn't White enough?

After morosely tossing these questions back and forth in his head, in April of 1964 Ray finally received a call to come in for an interview with the NYPD on the 18th of that month.

Ray pulled up to the New York Police Department in his best suit and with his curls slicked back. Although nerves had kept him up the entire night and he hadn't slept a lick, Ray knew better than to let them see him sweat. He swaggered into the building with a confident smile and a black coffee in his hand, as if he already belonged. "Good morning miss, my name is Raymond Wood and I'm here for an interview. I'll tell you what, you're lookin' at NYPD's newest officer right here." Ray purred to the receptionist, with a gleam in his chocolate brown eyes.

The receptionist rolled her eyes and asked him to take a seat in the waiting room. A few minutes later she returned and led Ray into a moderate sized office. She closed the heavy mahogany door with a slight click, indicating the start of his interview. After shaking hands and taking his seat, Ray was peppered with a fusillade of questions. There were many expected questions inquiring about his youth, his time in the military, and his last few years in New York. But he was also asked about a few unexpected topics.

Leaning forward on his elbows, the gruff interviewer asked, "What do you know about CORE or any of those kinds of groups?"

Ray was thrown off. In preparation for his interview he'd contemplated all kinds of questions they might ask and prepared calculated answers, but he wasn't prepared for this.

"Well, not much frankly. I've been in the city for about five years now, so I've heard about those groups, seen things on the news. Once I even went to some speech, but I was just there with some friends," Ray replied honestly. "That's about it."

They proceeded to show him a series of photographs and asked if he recognized anyone. The interviewer shuffled the photographs in front of him, giving him a few moments to review them. Ray perused the pictures, digging into his memory to see if he recalled any faces but he didn't recognize any of the people pictured.

Except for one.

"I recognize him," Ray said when he came upon one of the photos. "I don't know him very well, but he came to my apartment selling encyclopedias a while ago. He gave me some papers about some meeting he was holding, but I wasn't interested so I didn't give him much thought."

He wondered why they were asking him these types of questions and what did that encyclopedia salesman have to do with anything. Ray remembered him from their brief conversation, but he had only seen him on that one occasion. The interviewer then went on asking Ray more typical questions and the interview was back on track. And less than one hour after the receptionist had closed that door, Ray was up out of his seat shaking hands and accepting his on-the-spot job offer. He was offered a position in a new NYPD unit, the Bureau of Special Services and Investigations (BOSSI), a police surveillance squad that specialized in infiltrating, conducting countermeasures, and gathering intelligence on political and social groups. BOSSI paid special attention to civil rights, feminist, and anti-war protest groups (NYC Department of Information Records, n.d.).

During this time, the US government was undergoing serious efforts to combat Black activist organizations, dubbed "terrorist" groups, including the FBI's Counterintelligence Program (COINTELPRO). Organizations like BOSSI would provide information to COINTELPRO, using illegal measures to accomplish their aims (Rachell, 2019).

Ray was now a member of the NYPD's BOSSI unit.

May 1964

The NYPD wasted no time. Before Ray even had the opportunity to absorb what had just transpired, he was thrown right into the swing of things and started learning the ropes of police work. Wondering if perhaps he had oversold his confidence, Ray was immediately placed on assignment with no field training or even education on police procedure, much less any undercover training. He was given the cover of Ray Woodall, a 27-year-old Manhattan College at Fordham law student. He was placed undercover to infiltrate the Bronx chapter of one of the most prominent civil rights organizations in the country, the Congress of Racial Equality (CORE). CORE was the first Black activist group to promote nonviolence as the primary means to achieve racial equality. While the Bronx chapter was deemed the most militant of all the CORE chapters due to demonstrations they had arranged the previous year protesting employment discrimination, they still abided by CORE's ideology of nonviolence (Rachell, 2019).

Although Ray was slightly nervous about going undercover so soon after joining the force, he was ready to take on his role as Ray Woodall and prove himself as a cop. Ray thought back on the speech that he'd heard Malcolm X give the past year in Harlem. While he hadn't been paying much attention to the words due to his lack of interest in the topic at the time, coupled with his interest in the ladies,

Ray still remembered Malcolm X's strong presence, charisma, and the strength with which he spoke. It was impossible to ignore the passion and determination in his voice. When Ray went undercover as Woodall, he decided he'd try to emulate the master of charisma and command.

Dressed in a buttoned-down collared shirt and a pair of ironed slacks, Ray found it wasn't that difficult to step into his new persona. Aside from just the similarity of the names, Ray learned so much about the civil rights movement and the people involved, he soon found himself fully immersed in the role of Ray Woodall. Ray was a handsome, charismatic brother who soon rose the ranks to become CORE's housing chairman, coordinating a voter registration program (Felber, 2015).

Ray's assimilation into CORE was further expedited by a very important role that BOSSI had assigned to his Woodall persona. Woodall was going to be a small-time pot dealer. BOSSI supplied Ray with the funding to procure marijuana and advised him to start selling small quantities to the CORE members. Not only would Ray selling drugs explain why he had the kind of money that most Black men didn't have at that time, but it would also put him in a position to meet with many people from different chapters of CORE. BOSSI also provided Ray with plenty of alcohol and encouraged him to supply CORE meetings with liquor, simultaneously ingratiating himself with the crowd and enabling inebriation at CORE events. He would even host or bartend CORE rallies, securing his reputation as a "cool cat" while obscuring his true undercover identity.

Ray's appeal did not stop at camaraderie and paraphernalia contributor. He was a ladies' man, both beguiling with his charisma and attractive in his looks. Ray dated in and outside of CORE, both Black and White women. His romantic interludes weren't restricted to in person, either. Ray would write lyrical letters to a few female friends, finding the communication an escape from reality. By this time, he'd been spending a lot of his time undercover helping CORE lead protests and rallies and found himself needing brief respite from the weight he was starting to feel constantly pressed against his chest. Ray was starting to feel two-faced, having fun and befriending the same people he'd later snitch on to his BOSSI supervisors. During the day he was an activist, spouting the ideology of CORE next to people he called "brother" and "sister.". At night, he would report back to his BOSSI supervisors, relaying everything that he'd seen and heard.

One of the correspondences that helped momentarily alleviate his mind from the growing guilt was later discussed in a newspaper article. They recalled Ray's communication with a young lady. "Nice, chatty letters from a New York Negro involved in CORE to a pretty white acquaintance on a Mississippi summer project. 'Dear Miss Blood and Guts,' he wrote in an even hand, 'Take care of yourself down there. Don't do anything rash…Mississippi is the whole United States of America…I'd like to take a rifle and go down and join you, but that's just daydreaming.' In one letter he enclosed some clippings of the summer's Harlem riots and offered his own eye-witness account: 'I have seen cops beating cowering Negroes in the streets of Harlem.'" (Brownmiller, 1965).

The memories from the riots that Ray participated in, referenced in that letter, would remain etched into his mind until the day he passed. The brutality and violence that he experienced at many these protests was incomprehensible. Ray had been raised to fear the police and always keep his eyes averted when around law enforcement. His Aunt Easter had hammered into him, "Be respectful to the White people. Don't talk back, don't give them any kind of look." He was taught to do the opposite of standing up to Whites, much less opposing the police. Ray was particularly daunted, and impressed, by what he was witnessing.

He witnessed masses of Black and White people standing up fearlessly to police officers, only to be ruthlessly beaten, hosed, and chased down by dogs. When Ray took part in the Harlem summer riots, he watched as women with children were violently thrown to the concrete and men were beaten with billy clubs, spat on, kicked and called racial slurs. And yet they persisted, refusing to give up on their vision. The passion behind the resonating chants was just as powerful as the violence used against them. He was so inspired that he eventually began to lead people in chants and freedom songs.

As Ray delved deeper into his undercover role as Woodall and established himself as a well-liked member within the civil rights group, his BOSSI supervisors increased the pressure for evidence that could help them discredit and permanently shut down CORE. The juxtaposition between his feelings about what was going on and the requirements of his job began to keep Ray in a constant turmoil. He sympathized with CORE's mission and the brothers and sisters fighting for the cause. Ray saw people who were passionate about achieving social justice and equal rights. They wished to end racial discrimination and disenfranchisement so that Black people could be given a fair chance to live and succeed in America. When Ray searched his innermost thoughts and feelings, he just couldn't muster the same hatred or disgust that his supervisors had when discussing the civil rights groups.

Ray began to see that he was inevitably going to lead these people to destruction; he was taking them straight into a bloodbath when they had been nothing but welcoming and passionate about their cause. A cause that he was struggling to not see as his own. As a Black man, he'd seen and experienced everything that CORE was fighting against, so how could he not feel conflicted?

The weight of this burden eventually got to be too much for Ray. CORE admittedly had many members with a criminal past and he witnessed misdemeanors being committed. Obviously, as the guy selling everyone weed and providing booze for the parties, people were not necessarily secretive around him, especially about illegal drug use. But aside from these minor acts, he genuinely wasn't finding any evidence of felonious, criminal wrongdoings. Ray refused to report something so trivial, and hypocritical, as people smoking dope. Unfortunately, this lack of information relay led to more pressure from BOSSI for him to provide something to bring down CORE. He was growing tired of the pressure coming from the NYPD to produce evidence that just wasn't there.

Ray decided to reach out to his handler, Ted, to find a way out of this situation. He dialed the all too familiar number on his land line one night, pointlessly hoping to catch his handler in a rare good mood. Ted picked up after four rings with a gruff, "What do you want?"

"Listen man, this is not what I signed up for. You told me tha…"

"Alright son. Relax now before you blow your top and forget about the grass and booze we caught you with," the handler interrupted with an arrogant drawl. Ray wanted to slam the phone down. "It'd be a shame if you got booked with all that."

The moment he knew he was trapped.

"What are you talking about, Teddy? Y'all gave me the dough for that, told me I had to blend in with the guys from CORE!"

"Oh yeah? Says who?" Ted chuckled. "Your time with BOSSI has been kept quiet, on account of us needing you undercover. You better get on with it before things turn on you."

Ray quickly understood the what Ted was saying. He'd heard of this type of coercion and blackmail happening to other brothers on the force, but he thought this case would be different. He'd only acted under the direction of his superiors and hadn't fully realized what he was getting himself into. But although he was upset about the situation, Ray was used to having to bottle up his feelings in order to do what he had to get done. His experience in the US Air Force had taught him that how he personally felt about a mission was irrelevant. It was his job to carry out the orders of his superiors or face the corresponding consequences. And this situation was no different.

Given no choice but to come to terms with the severity of his predicament, Ray started to focus on ways he could give his BOSSI bosses what they wanted. He hoped the sooner he was done with this, the sooner this would all be behind him.

After contemplating his options and putting his reservations to the side, Ray knew what had to happen.

July 1964

Ray continued working his way up the Bronx CORE hierarchy and eventually became somewhat of an advisor to the chairman, Herb Callender. Having worked undercover with CORE for a few months, Ray was under extreme pressure from BOSSI to produce an arrest. With the guidance of his handler, Ray came up with the idea to convince Herb Callender to trespass on government property, where the two of them would attempt a citizen's arrest on Mayor Robert Wagner. Ray and Callender had already discussed in length the Mayor's continued racial discrimination in construction projects and Ray knew he'd be able to push Callender into taking action.

BOSSI's goal behind this machination was to create an opportunity for the NYPD to publicly arrest Callender, sullying his name while simultaneously creating an opportunity to come up with any other charges. The plan came together just as he'd anticipated. Ray, Calendar, and the CORE co-chairman went to New York City's Town Hall and attempted to place the mayor under a citizen's arrest. The three men were, unsurprisingly, immediately arrested by security police officers as soon as they stepped on the scene. Not only was Callender arrested and his reputation destroyed, he was sent to a hospital for psychiatric observation.

Ray hadn't expected that. He knew he was setting Callender up, but he didn't think things would take this turn. Regardless, Ray had done his job. He thought now that his superiors were happy and his mission accomplished, he could become an official NYPD police officer and begin the usual line of work. Ray thought his undercover days were through and he'd would be able to retire his role as Woodall. But BOSSI wasn't done with Ray.

November 1964

The attempted citizen's arrest of the New York City Mayor generated a lot of national publicity and shined a spotlight on Ray Woodall. Seemingly overnight, Ray had gained a reputation as a radical and revolutionary activist fighting for the civil rights movement. Since Ray's cover had not been blown and his Woodall persona was now highly esteemed amongst the civil rights groups, he became an even more valuable asset to BOSSI. Any hope that Ray had of leaving the undercover world and moving on to other forms of police work vanished.

Instead of relinquishing his undercover duties, Ray was reassigned to a new undercover mission, infiltrating a radical civil rights group, the Black Liberation Front (BLF). BLF was a small, radical civil rights group started by its militant activist leader, Robert Steele Collier. Collier and the BLF were more extreme in accomplishing their mission for equality, believing violence could be a means to claiming back their human and civil rights. Although BLF was new and didn't yet have a large following, Collier was an important figure for BOSSI to monitor and keep in line due to their violent, radical nature.

Less than a month into his undercover mission within BLF, Ray and Collier finally met face to face on December 14th. The men were introduced by Paul Boutelle, the Black socialist leader of the Freedom Now political party. The men were at a rally for the Progressive Labor Movement at the Manhattan Ballroom when the introductions between Ray and Collier were made. Ray had met Boutelle earlier, before Ray had even stepped foot inside the NYPD station. Shortly after Ray had arrived in New York, Boutelle had knocked on the door of his apartment trying to sell him encyclopedias. At the time, Ray and Paul started chatting and Boutelle told him about the group Freedom Now, a small, very new Black activist group. He also gave Ray pamphlets and even invited him to join them at an upcoming meeting.

Ray ultimately didn't attend the meeting and hadn't necessarily given Boutelle much thought after their encyclopedia encounter, until later, when he was shown a picture of Boutelle at his interview with the NYPD. Ray identified him as a member of Freedom Now and described their chance encounter. He always wondered if that chance encounter was what helped seal the interview for him. Nevertheless, whenever Ray was around Boutelle, he was concerned their initial meeting could potentially give him away. When they had first met, Ray had introduced himself using his real name, Ray Wood, since he wasn't yet a cop. Ray hoped his last name was similar enough to his undercover name as to not give his true identity away. Luckily, the meeting went on without a hitch and Ray was now right on track with his infiltration mission.

Ray had been determined to make contact with Collier for a while now and he didn't want to let this opportunity go to waste. On that same night that he met Collier, Ray tried to sycophantically create favor with Collier by making himself useful. He offered to provide Collier with some research documents divulging information on the Cuban delegation. Collier was interested in and they agreed to meet the following day. From that point on, Ray's charm and utilitarianism helped the relationship grow into the semblance of a partnership. Collier and Ray began routinely meeting to discuss ways to increase the BLF following and how to raise funding for the newly formed organization, all while Ray channeled this information back to his superiors.

It was Ray's mission to take this influential militant leader down from the inside. While he'd done something similar with Callender and the mayor's arrest attempt, it was substantially different this time. Collier was a dangerous man who would not hesitate to act violently if he knew Ray was really an undercover officer. On top of that, due to Collier's violent tendencies, BOSSI was exceedingly determined to silence or undermine him. Knowing this, Ray continued forward with trepidation and calculated moves, gaining more and more of Collier's trust while they worked together on various projects.

Shortly after Ray's introduction to Collier, Ray saw the perfect opening.

January 19, 1965

One of Ray's routine duties as an undercover BOSSI agent involved reporting back to his handlers with any updates or new information, including logs of all meeting attendees. During one of these meetings, Ray handed over a report that included two names: Walter Bowe and Khaleel Sayyed. Bowe and Sayeed were active members of the militant Black nationalist group, Revolutionary Action Movement (RAM) which held close ties to Malcolm X and his new controversial Organization of Afro-American Unity (OAAU). Bowe and Sayyed were both young, Black males who'd attended Howard University. Bowe was working as a judo instructor and Sayyed was a 22-year-old who'd just taken a leave of absence from school (Viola Jr., 2017).

Both men were rapidly gaining recognition in the civil rights community. Because of this rising notoriety, when Ray's report including Bowe and Sayyed's names landed in his handler's hands, BOSSI quickly made them the objective of their next strategy. Ray didn't realize what those names would mean for his mission. Ray hadn't yet made the connection, but BOSSI was already aware that Sayyed was an important part of Malcolm X's internal security. The BOSSI and the FBI had been tapping into Malcolm X's phones, and through this surveillance, knew of Sayyed's connection to Malcolm X.

As crowd control security coordinator, Sayyed was essential to Malcolm X's security team. This connection would prove critical to BOSSI's ultimate plan.

When Ray's mission changed focus from Collier to Bowe and Sayyed, at the time he didn't realize what the true purpose was for this new strategy. Ray was simply told his mission was now to establish himself as these two men's comrade and skillfully persuade them into committing a crime that would remove them from the protest scene, an act that Collier's attorney would later argue constituted entrapment. The connection Ray hadn't yet made was that the NYPD and FBI had a dark plan in mind when they wanted these men, especially Sayyed, removed from the scene. As head of Malcolm X's event security, Sayyed was crucial to ensuring Malcolm's safety. Arresting Sayyed would remove him from Malcolm X's events, leaving Malcolm X vulnerable to any threats.

With this new plan in mind, Ray prompted Collier to arrange a meeting between the two of them, Bowe, and Sayyed so that they could all work together on their next project in the fight for equality. Collier arranged a meeting between the four of them that was to take place in his apartment on January 19th. The men planned to discuss new, radical ways they could bring attention to their cause.

After that meeting was scheduled, Ray scheduled his own private meeting with his BOSSI handler to apprise him of the new occurrences. They met at the BOSSI headquarters located on Liberty Street, a small store front in lower Manhattan near the former World Trade Center. During this meeting, Ray and his handler Ted discussed his next move.

Whenever Ray met with BOSSI, a third, silent participant was always present. This individual was there that day, as usual, dressed in a midnight black suit and shiny dress shoes. Ray could tell right away he was a G-Man. FBI agents had a different way of dressing than typical officers, and Ray was told early on to act as if the G-Man wasn't there. It was evident the guy was with the feds, not just NYPD.

"At this meeting on the 19th, I want you to get those radicals to do something huge. Get them to try to blow up our friend Miss Liberty," Ted said, perhaps thinking of the Statue of Liberty he'd seen on his way to this meeting. "I'd like to get 'em tied up in a federal crime so bad that they won't ever get out."

"Yea, I think I can get them riled up," Ray admitted, talking directly to Ted and ignoring the G-Man as advised. "They're about ready to do whatever they hear, if they think it'll help their cause."

When Wood, Collier, Sayyed, and Bowe met on January 19th, tensions were high as the men were eager to get started on creating a new plan of action. Bowe, Sayyed, and Collier started to toss ideas around, with suggestions ranging from new protest locations and pamphlet designs, to possible slogans they could put onto posters. With the Statue of Liberty bombing plot in mind, Ray waited for the right moment to suggest the radical idea to them. In the midst of an impassioned discussion about the injustices they faced on a daily basis, and the urgency they felt to make change, Ray made his suggestion.

"Listen up, I have an idea. It's a bit out there, but it would leave them with no choice but to hear what we have to say," Ray said, a conspiratorial glint in his eyes. "We need to do something huge, man, something that will really make an impact."

"Right on! What you thinking, Ray?" Collier trusted Ray and was excited to hear what he had to say. The two had spent a lot of time together in the last month and a half, so Collier was initially more open than Sayyed or Bowe to Ray's ideas.

"The White man loves to talk about America being the 'land of the free' and 'opportunity,'" Ray said sarcastically. He stood up, rallying the others with his enthusiasm. "They clearly ain't never been a brother. Everywhere we go, we're looked down on, beat down, not given the same chance as others. Our women aren't safe. Our men are locked up for nothing. Our kids have to fight ten times harder to get the same education the White kids are given! Land of the free? No!"

"Damn right!" Bowe agreed, while Sayyed and Collier nodded enthusiastically.

"Fuck their so-called freedom! Let's take down their Statue of Liberty!" Ray was pacing the room, gesticulating wildly with his hands. "Blow it up! Let's get rid of their fake symbol for the liberty that we don't have! "

Everything was quiet for a moment. They all looked around at each other, trying to gauge if Ray was serious. This suggestion was more extreme than anything they'd taken on at this point. Sayyed and Bowe were hesitant.

"Yeah okay, why not the Liberty Bell and the Washington Monument, too?" Bowe scoffed, not believing what Ray was saying.

"I don't know, man. That's real heavy." Sayyed said, rubbing at the back of his head. "I was in the SNCC at Howard. Violence isn't the way I want to make change."

The men discussed the bombing idea for a while, going back and forth on the merits and risks associated with the plan. At one point, Ray thought the Statue of Liberty idea was losing steam and tried to propose another violent idea that would still accomplish BOSSI's mission of arresting these men. Ray suggested they go to Harlem and do stick-ups; they could use force to scare people into realizing they were not ones to mess around with. This idea was quickly shut down by the others. They generally didn't want to use violence, especially aimed at random people in the street. The Statue of Liberty idea was back on the table and the discussion continued.

Collier was the first to see Ray's vision, immediately thinking of connections he had in Canada who could help them fulfill this mission by procuring dynamite. Still, Sayyed and Bowe were not yet on board. More discussion about possible plans followed, but still no one was able to think of anything better. Eventually Bowe sided with the Statue of Liberty idea and Sayyed followed suit shortly after.

Now that all the men were in agreement with the bombing plan, Ray knew they needed to move quickly. He didn't want them to become disillusioned or persuaded out of the idea, so he suggested they act immediately. Ray encouraged them all to visit Ellis Island and the Statue of Liberty, to get familiar with the territory and plan out in detail when and where the bomb should be detonated. The four men agreed to individually survey the Statue of Liberty at different dates and times, and then rendezvous to discuss what they learned on their trips. This sounded like a good plan to them, very organized and detailed. For Ray, it gave BOSSI the added advantage of ensuring that the men were surveyed and witnessed casing out the area, days before the bomb plot. Ray reported back to his supervisors, letting them know the plan to bomb the Statue of Liberty was coming together.

January 26, 1965

After the men completed their individual Statue of Liberty scouting trips, they met again on January 26th at Collier's apartment. They discussed their trips at length, describing what they'd seen and heard, and were able to come together with a plan for the exact time and place they'd plant the bomb. They also discussed their plan to procure the dynamite. During their initial meeting on the 19th, Collier had mentioned that he had contacts in Canada that could help them with their plan. Collier's girlfriend at the time, Michelle Saunier, was a radical Quebec separatist he'd met a while back in Cuba. Collier suggested he and Ray drive up to Canada to meet with Saunier, who would have a plan for acquiring the dynamite. After discussing the risks of this across-the-border mission, they put some safety measures in place, finally coming up with a strategy they felt would securely get them in and out of Canada. The trip would happen in 3 days, with Ray and Collier making the drive, while Sayyed and Bowe waited back in New York for the next phase of the plan.

On January 29th, Collier and Ray drove up to Montreal to meet with Michelle Saunier, who offered them her apartment while they were in town. Knowing that this was not a casual visit but instead a trip with a purpose, Saunier had already scheduled a meet up with Michelle Duclos, who met them at her apartment to discuss how they would get the explosives. Duclos was a twenty-six-year-old French Canadian national and member of a Quebecois terrorist organization. Collier and Duclos had met the previous November in New York.

At this meet up, Duclos explained her plan. She didn't have the explosives on her at the moment; instead, she suggested driving the explosives down to New York herself. They spent time discussing the logistics and timing of the plan before coming to an agreement. They had a date set for when Duclos would deliver the dynamite for their overzealous scheme to bomb the Statue of Liberty.

February 16, 1965

Ray had just shut his eyes when he received a phone call that abruptly woke him. He was asleep in his Bronx apartment located at 1640 Topping Avenue, trying to catch as much rest as he could. Ray was out late the previous night cruising the town and trying out some bars he'd heard about. He answered the phone in a daze.

"Hello?" Ray answered, stifling a yawn.

"Hi, it's Michelle Duclos," she replied. "I'm in town, meet me at the Colonial House as soon as you can," she said, rushing to get off the line.

Before she'd hung up the phone, Ray was wide awake and hurriedly stepping into his shoes. Duclos had driven almost 400 miles from Montreal to New York in her Rambler and Ray didn't want to keep her waiting. He grabbed the first taxi he could find and told the driver to take him to the Colonial House Hotel.

When Ray arrived at the Colonial House, he found Duclos waiting for him and it was straight to business. She informed him that she'd successfully smuggled 30 sticks of dynamite and 30 blasting caps across the border. She'd hidden the explosives at a certain parking lot and explained in detail how he could get to it. As she traced her gloved finger along the hotel wall, she mapped out the path he'd take to find the package.

"When you get to the edge of the parking lot, there's a double fence marking the boundary." She looked him directly in the eyes, making sure he followed what she was saying. "Once you pass this fence, you'll see a bush in the adjacent empty lot. There's a Benjamin Moore paint box under this bush containing the dynamite."

"And the caps?" Ray asked. He liked her straight to the point attitude and the clarity with which she was depicting the scene.

"The blasting caps are wrapped in newspaper, hidden under the fourth car in the main parking lot." With her final instruction given, Duclos left and went back to her own hotel.

Immediately following his meeting with Duclos, Ray was met outside of the Colonial House by his handlers. He succinctly debriefed them on the information Duclos had just given him regarding the location of the explosives. He was then given a rental car so he could carry out the rest of the plan. With a car at his disposal, Ray called Collier to tell him he knew where the explosives were, and that he was on his way to pick him up so they could go get the packages.

Ray and Collier drove through the semi-dark February morning uptown through Manhattan, towards the Bronx. When they arrived at the large parking lot that Duclos had described, both men got out of the car. Collier passed the double fence and headed directly to the bush that held the paint box with the explosives.

"Got it!" Collier said to Ray as he carefully carried the box full of explosives to the car. Collier tried to hand Ray the box.

"No man, just place it in the car." Ray protested.

Within moments of putting down the box, they were surrounded. NYPD detectives and FBI agents swarmed the parking lot, rushing in from hidden positions and descending upon the two men. The police officers immediately seized the dynamite and found the blasting caps hidden in the snow under a parked car, exactly where Duclos said they'd be. Collier was arrested and Ray's undercover status no longer a secret to him. Collier was taken away in a police car, gaping at Ray in disbelief until he could no longer see him.

After Collier's arrest at the scene, the FBI went on to arrest the other known conspirators identified by Ray. Michelle Duclos was taken into custody at the Hotel Excelsior. FBI Special Agents then moved to arrest Khaleel Sayyed at the Go-Rite Deli in Brooklyn where the twenty two-year old worked and Walter Bowe was arrested at his home (Viola Jr., 2017).

The three men would face trial months later, while Duclos pleads guilty, for conspiring to destroy government property and smuggling explosives into the United States. Ray would go on to falsely testify at this trial, claiming that the Statue of Liberty idea, as well as the Harlem stick-up idea and proposition to scope out the Statue of Liberty beforehand, was solely initiated by Bowe, Sayyed, and Collier. During the trial, as well as the following appeal, Bowe, Sayyed, and Collier all adamantly testified that Ray was the one who brought the idea to the group and pushed them into action (Justia, 1966).

In the days following the arrests for the Statue of Liberty foiled bomb plot, Ray was promoted to detective 2nd grade and told he would no longer go undercover. He would begin training to as an NYPD detective. Despite the conflicting emotions Ray was feeling about the Statue of Liberty arrests, he was ecstatic to be done with undercover work. Collier now knew who he really was, and a photo of Ray had even made it into the news, though it only revealed a partial view of his face. Ray was glad his undercover identity had been blown! He thought this meant it was all over. Even his company commander, Tony Bouza, assured Ray that part of his life over. After a stressful and eventful week, Ray was ready to settle into his apartment in the Bronx for a weekend of rest, before beginning his first week of official police training.

February 21, 1965

On the morning of Sunday, February 21st, less than five days after the Statue of Liberty bomb plot, Ray was startled awake by an unexpected phone call. The caller had a brusque, unfamiliar voice and spoke with the authority of someone that expecting obeyance. Before Ray had time to question the voice on the line, the caller recited the secret contact code that only his BOSSI supervisors had knowledge of. Ray abruptly sat up in bed and started listening with tense attention.

"Leave your apartment and go downstairs. Go around the corner and get in the back seat of a black, Buick four-door vehicle."

Sensing the caller's urgency, Ray threw on the clothes he was wearing the night before and raced outside. As soon as he rounded the corner, he spotted the vehicle and reached for the door handle, a million questions racing through his mind. Ray's undercover identity had been blown almost a week prior, and he hadn't heard from BOSSI about any kind of upcoming mission. Not only that, but who was that on the phone? It certainly wasn't his handler Ted. And it certainly wasn't Ted waiting for him in the car.

As he entered the vehicle, he was greeted by two serious, White faces. Ray recognized one of the men as the silent agent who was always present during his meetings with Ted at the BOSSI headquarters. The G-Man had never spoken a word to Ray, much less met with him without Ted being present. The other man in the car was unfamiliar to Ray and his looming presence put Ray even more on edge. He guessed the guy was another G-Man, dressed in a slick back suit.

"Glad you could make it," the G-Man from the BOSSI meetings grunted sarcastically.

"What's this about?" Ray demanded. "Where's Ted?"

"We gave you the code so Ted doesn't need to be here. We need you to go over to the Audubon Ballroom over in Washington Heights," the G-Man continued. "We just want you to go inside and check it out. Should be easy enough."

"Today? But those cats already know who I am. What am I going over there for?" Ray didn't understand why they'd want him there, with people who knew him as Woodall. Ray wasn't even sure who "they" was. *Where was Teddy and why wasn't he the one giving him these instructions?*

"All of you Blacks look the same, they ain't gonna notice you," the no-named man spoke for the first time. Even though Ray was used to being talked to in this way by men like him, his fists couldn't help but clench in response. "Besides, only the side of your face was shown in that news photo."

"We don't have another one of you to send out there right now," G-Man added. "Just do your damn job. Lay back and observe what's going on. Just report back to us what you see. You are by no means to interfere if shit goes down."

Accepting his orders, Ray got out of the car and had barely closed the door as the car sped away. *If shit goes down?* Ray didn't even know what that meant. He was given a new assignment, but it didn't appear to be a proper mission. Ray was suspicious about Ted not being at the meeting, and he knew the G-Man had some stake in whatever was going on, always at their meetings and receiving the same information that Ray reported to BOSSI. The thing was, he'd been given the code, so he *had* to carry out their orders- Go to the Audubon Ballroom to observe and report back on an event occurring there later that day. The event? Malcolm X was scheduled to speak, to announce plans for a new organization he was starting.

Ray had, of course, heard of Malcolm X at this point. He'd even attended a handful of his events over the past couple of years. His name had been circulating in the civil rights scene for a while now, with talk of his radical ways spreading like wildfire. He was increasing in popularity as well as notoriety. Even if Ray hadn't been a part of the civil rights groups under his cover alias, he surely would've heard of Malcolm X through the news media. Malcolm X had just experienced an eventful year and a half, having taken his pilgrimage to Mecca, yet also facing difficulties with the Nation of Islam and Elijah Muhammed (CMG Worldwide, 2021). In this time frame Malcolm also visited Africa and established the OAAU, all while being under the surveillance of the government.

Malcolm X's crowd of supporters kept growing in numbers and strength; despite of and because of this, the government and police were wary of his rising influence.

The plan seemed simple enough, just observe and report. Ray did plenty of that during his time undercover, but he figured the higher ups must really be low on options if they wanted him there just days after the Statue of Liberty arrests. He did, however, concede that the no-named man had a point; his whole face had not been shared yet with the public, only a side shot. He knew there weren't many other brothers working for the NYPD, and a White officer at the Audubon would stick out like a sore thumb. Figuring this was explanation enough, Ray put his worry aside (as he often found himself doing with his police work) and went back to his apartment to change.

Ray arrived at the front of the Audubon Ballroom, taking in all the men and women bustling in and out of the building. The event was packed, with people talking excitedly about the speech Malcolm X was about to give. Ray immediately noticed the atmosphere was different than it usually was at these types of civil rights movement events, more tense and frazzled. He was surprised that he didn't see the usual organized security that patrolling the venue, especially since Malcolm X was in attendance. Malcolm's growing recognition necessitated strong security measures, especially at a large, anticipated event such as this one.

Ray was able to walk right in through the front door, with no body check for any kind of weapon or camera. He chose a seat in the front of the room, looked around, and noticed there were no police officers either, even though at least a handful of uniformed policemen were usually present at these rallies or gatherings.

Initially, Ray thought about attributing this difference to Malcolm X's recent spiritual journey; he thought that perhaps Malcolm was taking on a philosophy of nonviolence and didn't want to appear overly militant with extreme security measures. But Ray quickly discarded that theory after recalling a conversation with Sayyed a few weeks back.

While they planned the Statue of Liberty bombing, Sayyed told Ray he was helping Malcolm with security. He said he was now overseeing Malcolm's event security coordination. Sayyed said this with a proud smile, happy about the responsibility that he'd been given. At the time, Ray viewed Sayyed as so young and inexperienced, he hadn't realized the authority Sayyed truly had over Malcolm X's security team.

That explained it, Ray thought. Sayyed oversaw the coordination of security at Malcolm X's events, but he was still detained from the Statue of Liberty arrest five days ago. The only reason Malcolm would allow his security to be so lax was if something disrupted the usual flow of things.

As Ray sat in the front of the ballroom, contemplating the events of the past months and connecting the dots, his thoughts were interrupted by a loud noise at the back of the room. All heads turned towards the commotion; Malcolm had just stood up on stage, and his attention, too, was focused on commotion. As Malcolm tried to calm the crowd, Ray thought to himself, *This must be the shit going down like they were talking about earlier.* Suddenly, Ray heard a man shout, "Get your hands out of my pocket!" followed by the reverberation of gun shots blasting nearby.

Ray had been on high alert all day, having been abruptly woken that morning with the orders for this grim mission. Poised to move quickly, he bolted out of his seat and headed for the closest side exit door, adrenaline pumping through his veins. As he made his way through the confused, panicked crowd, Ray glanced back towards the stage. Amidst overturned chairs and splintered wood, Malcolm X was laid out on the stage, bleeding from each bullet wound he'd just been dealt.

Ray didn't have time to stop.

He raced out of the Audubon Ballroom, determined to get out as quickly as he could. Pushing his way towards the exit, out of the corner of his eye he saw a man drop something. *It was a damn shotgun!* Ray slowed his pace and, contemplated approaching the man to try and take the gun away so he couldn't hurt anyone else. But remembering the G-Men's advice from earlier, Ray decided to follow commands and not interfere.

Ray made his way outside, overhearing the havoc and chaos occurring inside as a result of the barrage of bullets. He was barely a few steps out of the building when someone yelled out, "Grab that son of a bitch!" Just then a man seized Ray by the shoulder.

"Get off of me!" Ray shrugged out of the stranger's hold, scrambling to get away from the growing throng of people.

As Ray tried to escape from the vengeance of whatever the crowd thought that he had done, he was roughly apprehended by a uniformed officer. The officer put Ray in handcuffs and dragged him into the back of a patrol car. Bystanders looked on as he was driven away, bright lights and sirens racing towards the precinct.

Ray struggled in the back, shuffling in the seat trying to sit up while his hands were cuffed at his back. "What's going? Why did you cuff me?"

Ray's questions were met with silence. He debated telling the unhelpful officer he was actually an undercover officer and demanding answers. But as soon as the thought crossed his mind, Ray dismissed it. Whatever was going on, the less he knew the better. Something bad had just gone down and Ray didn't know what he should be saying or to whom.

Ray could hear the police radio, firing off information about the scene at the Audubon. Gloom settled in the pit of his stomach. His mind kept percolating over the events of the last year and earlier today, putting together all the loose ends he couldn't believe he hadn't picked up on before. Ray knew his time undercover was spent aiding the police in missions that were less than holy, but he never imagined his actions would start the domino effect leading to today's events.

Ray spent the next three hours in a holding cell at the precinct jail with his arms crossed, alternating between pacing the room and sitting on the cold metal bench. He mulled over the thousands of thoughts and questions rolling around in his head, hoping to come up with an explanation that was less sinister than what just transpired. *Malcolm X getting shot today at the Audubon Ballroom never would've happened if there had been more security, like there usually was at these events. BOSSI was so insistent that I get Sayyed arrested less than a week ago, it can't be a coincidence. And they sent me to the ballroom this morning, knowing that something was going to go down!*

Ray felt a headache coming on that he was afraid would never go away.

As Ray's eyes drifted shut with exhaustion, he was finally let out of the cell by a guard with a permanently bored look on his face. Also at the door to the cell were the same two G-Men he'd met earlier that morning. They put Ray back into handcuffs and led him in silence towards the rear exit of the building, where an unmarked vehicle was waiting for them. This was the last detail that fully convinced Ray that these White guys were G-Men.

"What the fuck, man?" Ray asked as soon as they were in the car. He didn't have the patience for fake pleasantries. He needed information, now. "What went down today?"

The once silent G-Man stepped on the gas and they sped away from the precinct. “Don't worry about it. You did what we asked and that’s all you should be concerned about.”

“But I don’t know what it was that I did!” Ray exclaimed. “I went into the Audubon and everything was pretty normal at first, except they didn’t have any security.” The two men in the front looked at each other, exchanging a silent message. “As I was running out of the building, I saw a man with a shotgun.”

“Did you speak to him?” the other man asked, speaking to Ray for the first time since picking him up from the jail.

“No. I thought about stopping him, but you guys told me to just watch, not interfere,” Ray added quickly, not wanting to get in any trouble for breaking protocol.

“Did anyone see you?” the first G-Man asked.

“Yeah, once I was outside someone recognized me and grabbed me,” Ray responded. “Right before the police cuffed me. What was that even about, me getting arrested? No one told me that was a part of the plan.”

"That doesn't concern you anymore. It's been taken care of," he told him. "Forget you were ever there, forget you even spoke with us. You did your part, now get outta here. And lay low for a while."

Ray got out of the car and made his way to his apartment, his bones weighing him down due to everything he'd been through that day. When Ray entered his apartment, the first thing he did was fill a glass with Scotch and turn on the TV. He listened as reporters announced that Malcolm X had been shot at the Audubon Ballroom. He watched as people rioted and mourned in the streets. Ray slumped down onto his couch, overcome by the remorse gripping his lungs, making him feel like he was going to suffocate.

Malcolm X was dead. And Ray played a part in it.

For many endless weeks, Ray stayed mostly indoors, leaving only for essential trips to the grocery store and the academy police training he was finally going through. From his small apartment, he listened to the news and learned all the new information coming out about Malcolm X's death.

On the day of Malcolm X's assassination, Thomas Hagan was arrested while fleeing the Audubon. A few days later, a man named Norman Butler was also arrested, followed by the arrest of a third suspect, Thomas Johnson, a few days after that .The three men were all members of the Nation of Islam and were arrested for their collaboration in the murder of Malcolm X. Butler and Johnson always claimed their innocence, and Hagan went on record stating the two played no role in Malcolm X's assassination (Bates, 2020).

When Ray saw a photo of Thomas Johnson, he was shocked. *That man looks like me!* Ray hadn't seen him at all that day at the Audubon and he couldn't shrug off the uncanny resemblance, nor the way the G-Men had told him that his arrest had been "taken care of."

Ray felt he knew so little about what happened, yet he knew so much more than what the media was saying. He knew that the NYPD was involved in the coordination of Malcolm X's murder and the FBI also play a role in the whole scheme. He knew he'd also played role in his assassination, beginning from the Statue of Liberty plot that was coordinated in order to get Sayyed, Bowe, and Collier arrested. Those arrests ultimately led to Malcolm X not having the security that could have potentially protected him on that fateful day in the Audubon Ballroom. And Ray also knew he had been sent to the Audubon Ballroom on direct orders from the G-Men on behalf of BOSSI, and more than likely the FBI, on the morning of February 21st, under their full knowledge something catastrophic was going to happen that day.

Ray was devastated. He should've realized this sooner.

After the Statue of Liberty trial, Ray's cover was essentially blown. He received a lot of attention from the media as well as from the NYPD. To the public eye, Ray was an undercover officer who'd stopped a radical civil rights group from committing a terrorist attack against a national monument. However, Ray was the guy who actually incited this act, not the other men. Regardless, Ray received a barrage of commendations for the bravery he showed that day, including a Hero's Award and a Medal of Valor.

The Statue of Liberty news even reached Ray's hometown of Chester, South Carolina. After it broke back home, his old high school awarded Ray a high school diploma along with that year's graduating class. Since the public had no idea he was there that dreadful day at the Audubon, aside from the few people claiming to have seen him there, Ray was honored for his valiant behavior. The world was blind to the horror he'd been a part of.

(Photo of Ray Wood receiving an award; 1965)

Part Three

Present Day

When Ray told me his story, he described the overpowering anxiety and inner turmoil he felt while waiting it out in his apartment, laying low until the day of the Statue of Liberty trial. He'd been exposed to an onslaught of novel experiences during those two years working undercover as Ray Woodall; he'd experienced the rush of the civil rights movement, multiple riots, protests, arrests, a bomb plot, and even a trip to Canada. Yet he still felt completely inexperienced when it came to undercover detective work.

At barely 30 years old, Ray had not received any training before being thrown into this undercover role. He was a Rookie with zero police skills when he was thrust into the heinous machinations of the NYPD. Yet Ray couldn't help but be ashamed it had taken him that long to understand what was really going on. BOSSI had shown him early on they didn't care about him. They were willing to break the law, blackmail, and manipulate him. But despite the moral turpitude that they'd displayed thus far, Ray had been blind to their ultimate dark scheme- To arrest Sayyed so Malcolm X would be unprotected and vulnerable to an attack. Ray spent countless hours ruminating over everything that occurred over the past two years, dismayed about his prominent role in these historical events.

Ray had befriended people and gotten to know people on a personal level, only to feel like he was later betraying them. That's how Ray felt about Sayyed and Bowe, especially when walking into the Statue of Liberty trial. Not only did Ray have strict orders from his supervisors about what his testimony should reveal, but he felt he was now in too deep to be able to walk away unscarred. Ray had become so involved in whatever the NYPD had orchestrated, there was no way for him to back out now without implicating himself. An undercover agent should only witness and report on crimes being committed by others, not instigate, coerce, or entrap others into committing a felony. That's exactly what Ray knew he'd done, not only to the Statue of Liberty defendants Collier, Sayyed, and Bowe, but also to Herb Callender when he convinced him to perform a citizen's arrest on the mayor. Ray had played a crucial role in incarcerating and tarnishing the reputation of these individuals, all while under the instruction of BOSSI.

Ray went on to testify as chief witness at the Statue of Liberty trial, falsely stating that Bowe was the one who conceived the bomb plot, while Sayyed had thought of the Harlem stick-up ideas. During the trial, Bowe and Sayyed refuted Ray's testimony saying these ideas both emanated from Ray (Justia, 1966). In Ray's conversations with me as well as in his signed confession letter, he admits that this was a false witness and he lied that day in court to comply with his supervisor's directions to not implicate himself. Ray was indeed the one to not only think of this plot, but he put a lot of energy into convincing these men to go along with it.

When the Statue of Liberty case was over, Ray's career in the NYPD continued. Ray worked for the NYPD until he retired in 1985, then went to work as a social security investigator. Ray's detective career was kickstarted in 1964 with his undercover role of Ray Woodall and that was only the beginning. Ray's undercover police work in the civil rights world was far from over.

Ray's time undercover as Ray Woodall created an opening for him within the civil rights movement that the police department wouldn't let go to waste. The 60's and 70's were a completely different era, with no social media and very limited photography, therefore Ray's appearance in photos was barely a deterrent in the NYPD's mission to infiltrate, discredit, and halt the civil rights organizations, which they referred to as "terrorist groups." Additionally, there were very few Black men in the police force at the time, so people generally didn't suspect Ray of being a police officer. They typically looked instead at White people in the civil rights scene for signs of possible surveillance.

Ray didn't want to just leave the police force, either. The salary he made as a police officer was rare for a Black man during that time, in any profession. No other "legal" job would make him that kind of money. So, despite Ray's hopes that his work undercover was finished and he would now be a regular detective, his undercover role continued until 1971. Ray went on to interact with groups such as the Revolutionary Action Movement (RAM) and the Black Panthers.

Ray's story continued long after that dreadful day at the Audubon Ballroom.

(Photo of Ray after retirement in 1985; Family photograph)

The shame Ray felt over manipulating all these people was overwhelming, and the guilt over what the plot ultimately led to was all-consuming. Ray hadn't realized it beforehand, but what was now clear to him was that BOSSI had been adamant about getting Sayyed arrested because they wanted to weaken Malcolm X's security detail. Less than a week following the arrests, Malcolm X was assassinated. This meant Ray was an essential part of the plan that created the opportunity to kill Malcolm X. While Ray was deeply forlorn about his own involvement, he was even more terrified by what this said about the police. They helped orchestrate the assassination of an influential Black civil rights leader and used Ray as a pawn in their plan.

The suspicious timing between the arrests and the assassination did not go by unnoticed by certain historians, researchers, and journalists. Many who have researched the assassination of Malcolm X have warily noted the implications of these coincidental occurrences. In a Black studies document written in 1979 discussing the Revolutionary Action Movement, the author states Khaleel's arrest disrupted Malcolm X's security and created a tone in the public environment that facilitated conspiracy (Ahmad, 1979).

Not only did the timing of those two events raise suspicions, but Ray's particular involvement in both the Statue of Liberty plot and the assassination was also noticed and has been studied in the last decade. In 2015, an historian was researching the assassination of Malcolm X and came across a document recently released by the FBI. The historian, Garret Felber, wrote the article "Malcolm X assassination: 50 years on, mystery still clouds details of the case," which discussed Ray and an eyewitness account found in these newly released documents. The personal papers of James Campbell, an activist who helped found the Liberation School, revealed a note written by Japanese American activist Yuri Kochiyama (below). The meeting notes from March 6, 1965 report that Ray Wood was sighted leaving the Audubon Ballroom on the day of the assassination (Felber, 2015).

(Ray Woods is said to have been seen also running out of Audubon; was one of two picked up by police. Was the second person running out)

('Ray Woods is said to have been seen also running out of Audubon; was one of two picked up by police. Was the second person running out.') (Felber, 2015)

When this article came out in 2015, Ray caught wind of the news. He panicked. At that point, Ray hadn't been discussed in the media since the 70's, and he was worried what this would mean for his safety. When his time undercover officially ended, Ray had witnessed and participated in so many suspicious and dark events, he was terrified of discovery. He knew Felber's theory was correct- he *was* at the Audubon Ballroom that day, on orders. Ray feared the police, the FBI, and the public. He'd spent years living in relative obscurity, wanting to ensure the cops wouldn't preemptively act to silence him. He also feared retribution from society, especially the Black community. Ray was ashamed of what he'd been a part of and felt he'd betrayed his own people. Due to his lugubrious feelings about his actions and fear for what might be done to him in retaliation, this 2015 article deeply impacted Ray. He subsequently ensconced himself in his home, away from family yet again.

Deep down, he felt it wouldn't be long until the truth came out.

After he saw Felber's article, Ray called while I was driving. I tapped the Bluetooth and said, "Hey Ray, what's going on, man?" I hadn't seen the article and thought he was calling about upcoming plans we had with the family.

"You know, same ol' same ol'," Ray sighed, his voice resonating in the vehicle. "Well, actually not really. I'm calling to let you know I won't be able to make the barbeque at your house this weekend."

"Yeah, no problem. Is everything okay? You sound kind of down."

"I'm not really down, just want to be safe. It's hot for me right now and I don't really want to be seen. I especially wouldn't want your family to get caught in the crosshairs of this whole thing."

"What do you mean?" I asked him, starting to get concerned. He was being very cryptic and sounded resigned. He seemed ready to succumb to whatever was bothering him.

"You're one of the few who already know something about this, so I feel I can talk to you. But would you mind if we met to talk about it?"

We decided to meet later that day so that he could tell me what was going on. By this time, I'd already heard Ray's story at length and knew about his time as an officer and everything he'd done. I understood his reluctance to talk on the phone and wasn't even surprised that he didn't want to spend time with the family anymore. Ray had spent most of his adult life dolefully ashamed of what he'd been a part of and afraid it would one day come back to haunt him. As a result of this fear, he was constantly relocating and isolating himself. I was one of the few people who understood this aspect of Ray's character. Some people saw him as a loner, someone who preferred their own company instead of large groups. But it was his shame and fear holding him back from fully opening to others. I knew Ray's mind was tormented by his past and he wished to be expunged of the guilt after he died, when he could no longer be castigated for his actions.

When I arrived at Ray's house, the somber mood rolled like a fog across his living room. He was sitting on the couch, the dim light of the muted TV offering dancing shadows in the room. I flicked on the overhead light and sat down next to Ray. He went and got his computer, then pulled up Felber's article.

"It's been so long since someone mentioned my name and Malcolm X's name in the same sentence. Someone called and told me they saw my name in this article. Look, Reg." Ray scrolled down the article and showed me the document putting Ray at the scene of the Audubon.

"Now this isn't the first time I've been talked about suspiciously in the news, but this is different. It's been years since anyone talked about this and now there's written proof I was seen there the day that Malcolm died," Ray glanced worriedly at me, looking for some kind of comfort.

“I understand why you’d be worried about this, Ray, but people have theorized about the police being involved in Malcolm X’s assassination for years now.”

This was true. There has been much speculation regarding law enforcement’s infiltration and involvement in many dubious activities during the civil rights movement, not just the murder of Malcolm X. As a law enforcement agent, Ray acted on behalf of the police during his infiltration of many different civil rights groups. Ray’s NYPD instruction, reinforced by the G-Men, was to infiltrate these so-called “terrorist” groups and incite crime, capture information, and report back. This was exactly what Ray had done in his early missions. He coerced and manipulated Sayyed, Bowe, and Collier into attempting the Statue of Liberty bombing and he incited Herb Callender into attempting the citizen’s arrest on the Mayor of New York City.

Both of these events that created and incited by Ray as a detective were detrimental to the cause not only because they led to the incarceration of men participating in the civil rights movement, but also because they sullied the name of these organizations in the eyes of the public. In a 2019 news article by historian L.E.J. Rachell discussing law enforcement involvement with Black radical groups, the author stated, “Wood was not just spying on CORE but was on a mission to ‘misdirect, disrupt, discredit and neutralize’ CORE's leadership… Such operations demonized Black leaders in the public eye and thereby de-legitimized both the Civil Rights and Black Power movements (Rachell, 2019)."

Police involvement and malfeasance against the Black community was rampant during Ray's career as a police officer and continues haunting our community. Malcolm X's assassination has been a conundrum many theorists have attributed to police involvement, yet this had never been proven. But now, Ray corroborates this theory in the detailed account you read here. In his signed confession letter, he admits that the police conspired to assassinate Malcolm X by arresting Sayyed, then sending Ray out to the Audubon on that fateful day.

Ray also admits in this account that the NYPD planted him as an undercover agent into these civil rights groups, to encourage and incite them to commit crimes. This permitted the police to arrest members of these groups, thereby discrediting them. Ray's involvement with Callender in the citizen's arrest of the mayor, and also with the Statue of Liberty plot, attests to the lengths law enforcement agencies were willing to go to derail the civil rights movement. Through BOSSI, the NYPD commanded Ray to go undercover and infiltrate various civil rights groups, citing them as dangerous terrorist groups. It's impossible not to notice that White supremacy groups, such as the KKK, did not qualify as "terrorist groups," despite the atrocities the group has perpetuated for decades in America.

Ray's admission is indicative of a law enforcement agency corrupted by an inherent bias and racism towards people of color. During his career from 1964-1985, Ray participated in despicable acts, including the assassination of Malcolm X, that kept him living in shame and remorse for his entire life. This book provides record of what he witnessed and participated in during his time as an NYPD police officer.

The brutality and horror of what he'd helped the police do haunted him perpetually and his dismay was exacerbated during the last few years of his life when the issue of police brutality and corruption against minorities once again moved to the front and center of America. Seemingly endless murders committed against unarmed Black people by police officers, officers who are paid by citizens' tax dollars to serve and protect, have propelled the Black Lives Matter movement to the forefront of society in recent years. Too many lives have been taken at the hands of police officers who will almost never face any real consequence or legal retribution.

On March 13, 2020, Breonna Taylor, an unarmed, 26-year-old EMT in Louisville, Kentucky, was shot and killed by plainclothes cops in her own bed while laying next to her boyfriend. The police burst into her home unannounced with a "no-knock" search warrant, supposedly looking drugs from an ex-boyfriend. No drugs or any other illegal substances were found.

George Floyd, an unarmed Black man in Minneapolis, Minnesota, was murdered on May 25, 2020, when an officer with a long history of abuse knelt on his neck, in broad daylight, in front of many onlookers, until he stopped breathing. Within a few days, most of America had watched the horrific nine-minute video. We heard him use his last dying breath to plead "I can't breathe," while other officers stood idly by, watching the life leave George Floyd's eyes.

Elijah McClain, a 23-year old Black man living in Aurora, Colorado suffered from cardiac arrest on August 24, 2019, after being thrown to the ground by police and injected with ketamine. He was walking home from the store, after buying his brother an iced tea. America heard his last words as he pleaded to the officers, "I am an introvert. Please respect the boundaries that I am speaking." He was removed from life support on August 30, 2019.

Those are just three names. Three out of the countless many lives taken too soon by police officers, who acted as judge, jury, and executioner in one broad stroke.

Tamir Rice

Botham Shem Jean

Philando Castile

Sandra Bland

Michael Brown

...

Five more names. If I were to list all the men, women and children whose lives have been taken by police over the last decade, the list would inherently be incomplete. How many more stories like Ray's, where police murder a Black person in cold blood, with no repercussions, are hiding in other American souls?

Ray's final years on this Earth were spent percolating through all the guilt festering in him since the day he joined the NYPD. The shame, guilt, and resentment boiling within him since then was only kept at bay by an even greater fear and paranoia that immobilized him. I wish that Ray had been brave enough to share his story with the world while he was alive. His attestation to the malfeasance and corruption existing in the NYPD, and most likely the FBI, calls for further investigation into police corruption during that time. Here's proof that it exists. Ray's testimony has the potential to exonerate people wrongfully convicted. It sheds light on the dark motives that drove BOSSI, and it confirms the stories of Herb Callender, Khaleel Sayyed, Walter Bowe, and Robert Collier. Ray was an undercover police officer who had explicit orders to derail and discredit specific civil rights groups. He was commanded by his superiors, the NYPD and the invisible hand that likely guided them, to be at the Audubon Ballroom to "observe" on the day of Malcolm X's assassination.

This testimony of prior police knowledge of, and involvement in, the assassination of Malcolm X partly answers the question, "Who Killed Malcolm X?" The NYPD had an active role in his assassination, and Ray's confession puts us on a path of finding out exactly what happened. Because now we know who was involved.

Although Ray's actions were ultimately guided by self-preservation, his choice to share his detailed story with me and his request that I share it with the world, was bravery. Like many other Black people throughout this country's history, Ray had to make sacrifices in order to get the same opportunities as others. He betrayed his people. He lied to them, faked who he was and relayed information back to the NYPD. But he also refused to report the drug misdemeanors to his supervisors. He tried, repeatedly, to get out of the situation he'd gotten himself into. And even when Ray knew what he was doing was woefully wrong, he wasn't fully aware of the extent of what was happening. Yes, Ray betrayed his people. But the NYPD also betrayed him.

I'm grateful that Ray had the bravery to not let his story go with him to the grave. He suffered because of his choices. He lived in fear, constantly moving around and refusing to form any real connections. Ray's funeral was sparsely attended, and he lived much of his life as a lonely man, secretly atoning for his sins and those of the NYPD. But Ray made sure I had the truth. He trusted me to share his story with all the detail, the emotion, and the trauma that he felt when living it. He entrusted to me his signed confession, knowing I would abide by his wishes.

Ray was complex, his inner workings a disproportionate maze formed by the experiences of his youth. Molded by the racism he saw play out throughout his entire life. He was cornered and trapped by his ill-informed decisions. Ray Wood wasn't faultless, by any means. He was just a Black man trying to make it in a world that was not designed for people of color to succeed.

Author's Note

For over nine years, I have known Ray's story and shared the burden of its weight with him until his passing, when the burden shifted solely onto my shoulders. My feelings have gone through a roller coaster of highs and lows over the years. There have been times I've thought about just not sharing this story at all. And then there were times I tried to convince Ray to share it himself, while he was still alive. But one thing that remained constant was Ray's desire to expunge himself of this secret after he was no longer here on this Earth.

I have shared with the world Ray's story. His life, his memories, his sin, and his remorse. Ray gave this knowledge to me, confident that I would do my best to honor his wishes and hold it until he was gone. When Ray initially told me his story, I didn't know what I was getting myself into. That night at his apartment I was wholly unprepared for the journey that would ultimately lead me here today.

I listened to what he was telling me, enraptured and horrified by its significance. As soon as I got home, I rushed to jot everything that he'd told me down onto the first paper I could find, one of my daughters' old composition notebook from school. I didn't know how much time Ray had left and how many more conversations we'd be able to have about this topic. He was an older man who'd already faced cancer once. We didn't know if he'd make it through that battle again.

I was thinking of how I'd be able to carry out the task that he'd given me for when he passed. I'd gotten so much information from him, on a story that I didn't yet fully know or understand. Luckily, for Ray and myself, we were given more time. Ray lived until November 24, 2020, and those years in between were used to give me the details of his past. I've used the same composition notebook I used that first night throughout the years, using it to write down the details of Ray's youth, his beginnings in New York, and his time with the NYPD. He told me about his introduction to undercover police work, how new and inexperienced he felt. He described his perspective and experiences. He told me how he felt back then and how he felt about it in the present. We shared laughs and we shared many tears.

Over the years that Ray shared the stories of his life with me, I was able to get to know and comprehend him on a deep level. I listened to the details of the attempted arrest on the NYC mayor with Herb Callender. He told me what happened that day and the conversations he had, with Callender and with BOSSI, leading up to that day. He described the Statue of Liberty bomb plot, his relationships with those people and how he manipulated them. Ray told me about February 21, 1965 and what he witnessed and participated in that day. I will never forget the tears that were streaming down Ray's face and the crack in his voice when he told me about being there at the Audubon Ballroom on the day that Malcolm X was murdered.

I share Ray's story in this book, now, remembering the emotion that overcame him during these conversations. But, despite the turmoil and trauma that Ray re-lived during each of these talks, he understood the importance of those conversations and shared that understanding with me. As Black people, our history in America has seen many dark times, as well as times of courage and strength. Especially in the last few years, America has had no choice but to come face-to-face with the institutional racism and corruption that has plagued our nation for centuries. Conversations like the ones I shared with Ray, and am sharing with the world now, are crucial to helping us repair the damage that has been done.

The significance of what Ray experienced as an NYPD officer is monumental when we talk about police corruption and the civil rights movement. To our family on a personal level, Ray's story has further motivated us to get more involved in the BLM movement. As a Black family, we see firsthand the injustices that our people face. The Wood family has seen tragedy and we have seen success. And although Ray's story is ultimately one that brings sadness, we can make his story also bring resolution and clarity to our community.

Over the last year, Ray's health was deteriorating, and we knew then that the time was soon coming. He was 87 years old and I knew that I should start preparing for what was to come. It was at this time that I told my youngest daughter, Breonna, about Ray's past and what I would have to do with the account of his past. As a young Black mother with a small daughter, Breonna is very passionate about the Black Lives Matter movement and I knew that she would be moved by Ray's story, too. When I described Ray's past to her, being the smart, tech-savvy millennial that she is, Bre was able to find many news articles and research documents that spoke about Ray. We looked those documents over together and realized that the country had been speculating about Ray Wood and his involvement in Malcolm X's assassination since it happened!

Those documents started me on the path of reading, researching, and investigating more about that time period. I reached out to my Goddaughter and one of Breonna's best friends, Lizzette, to help me put Ray's story into words that would justly and eloquently tell his account in a manner that would captivate the reader, as well as portray the complexity of his feelings. Together, I think that we have done that. We spoke to many historians and journalists who were gracious enough to talk with us, such as Susan Brownmiller, L.E.J.

Rachell, Garret Felber, Jake Halpern, Josh Davis, and Chenjerai Kumanyika. They were extremely helpful, providing information and directing us to other sources of information.

This book is Ray's eyewitness testimony of his participation as an undercover police officer in the events that led to Malcolm X's assassination.

Note from the Coauthor

I have been a friend to the Wood family for over ten years and am grateful for the opportunity to not only help write this story, but to learn about Ray Wood and everything he experienced back in that time. I knew Ray when I was a teenager and never would have imagined the dark history that he was a part of. At the time, I knew him only as the kind, older Wood relative that would often be at family events. I am sincerely appreciative that I was able to help Reggie tell the world Ray's truth.

As someone who has had a lifelong passion for reading, I wanted to help share this heartbreaking and complex story with skill and honesty. As a Latina American graduate student currently pursuing their Master's in Health Administration, with an interdisciplinary Bachelor's degree in Political Science and Criminology, I am honored to have been able to use the writing and research skills that I've gained throughout the years to help write this short memoir. I would like to thank my fiancé, Daniel, for supporting me and my involvement in this project, I love you. And thank you to my Mom for always supporting my love of literature.

-Lizzette Salado

Acknowledgements

First and foremost, I thank God for the blessings that He has bestowed upon my family and me. I thank Him for His grace and mercy. I thank Him for guiding me to do the right thing with the information that was placed into my care. I thank Him for leading Ray back to his family and blessing us with his kind and giving presence. When I was unsure about coming forward with this story, He reminded me that, "I can do all things through Christ who strengthens me." (Philippians 4:13). He is my witness. I will work for change and peaceful understanding.

Angela: Who knew those 33 years ago at the Ben Lomond Barn Community Center during my first DJ gig, I would meet my soulmate? You have towed the rope with my crazy ass for better or for worse. We have overcome so many challenges together. You believed in me when no one else did. You have always encouraged me to step out there and "just do it," but be the best at it or I'm going to hear about it later. Your no-nonsense, tough love style was what God knew that I needed in my life. I think that John Legend said it best in his song "All of Me." The many times that I wanted to quit working on this project you encouraged me to continue. I look forward to seeing your glitter and shine every day until God calls us home. I love you and I hope that I make you proud.

Breonna: My baby girl, my protégé, I can't say enough about how proud of you I am. Your help with research on this project was on point, your devotion to helping me confirm the facts of Ray's story was an eyeopener. It made me realize that you were serious about social justice and are a woman that stands for the truth no matter what the cost. You are amazing. I love you. Thank you.

Dad: WOW! Where do I start? When I was a very young boy, I sat on the parade field and watched you lead a group of young soldiers in drills. You had your neatly pressed uniform, polished black boots, and crisp baseball cap pulled down just above your eyes. You were yelling commands while everyone responded with a loud, "yes, sir!" I later asked why you were yelling at those men and you responded, “I’m saving lives son.” I still don’t know what that meant, but from that day on you were my action hero. My dad was Gi-Joe. I named my toughest army figure after you, “Get em’, dad, save the world.” When I was a child, you were my imaginary action hero and as an adult, you are my Sensei. Thank you for inspiring me to do great things. I love you, Dad.

Ashaad: My Godson, you have grown up to be quite a guy, you have always been there for me whenever I needed you. You're going to be an amazing actor. keep shining bro.

Lizzette: My Goddaughter, girl, we did it! I could not have done it without you! You are an amazing writer and I know that this is just the beginning! Use your platform and brilliance for the greater good, be bold, and let’s get into the fight. Change comes when someone decides to speak up. Let’s scream from the mountain tops, “Justice and equality are our human rights!”

Friends: David, Justin, Rassan, Alan, Stuart, Tarsha, Keith, Barbara, Gerald, Raheem and James. Thank You.

Cousin Ray RIP: It’s out! You can rest in peace now. Thank you for trusting me to do the right thing with your confession. I promise that I will use this platform for change. I remember us watching the Trayvon Martin trial together and you had this look of disgust on your face.

You went on about how f'ed-up the system was. Saying "J. Edger Hoover started this racist, calculated, corrupt, Jim Crow system of policing Black people! When does it stop?" At that time, I thought, *Who and what the hell is he talking about?* I am WOKE now, my friend. I will work to use your story and the 56 years of your guilt and suffering to make change. I will tell everyone who will listen. I will be a good student of the cause and try to find a way forward, to where change is real. RIP. November 24, 2020.

-Reggie Wood

Bibliography

Ahmad, Muhammad. (1979) *History of RAM - Revolutionary Action Movement.* Black Studies Document. Pages 26-27. Accessed December 1, 2020 from http://freedomarchives.org/Documents/Finder/DOC513_scans/RAM/513.RAM.History.of.RAM.pdf

Bates, Josiah. (2020, February 20) *The Enduring Mystery of Malcolm X's Assassination.* Time. Accessed December 1, 2020 from https://time.com/5778688/malcolm-x-assassination/

Brownmiller, Susan. (1965, June 3). *Statue of Liberty Case. View from the Inside: I Remember Ray Wood.* The Village Voice; Pages 3 & 11.

CMG Worldwide. (n.d.). *Malcolm X Biography.* Accessed December 1, 2020 from https://www.malcolmx.com/biography/

Felber, Garrett. (2015, February 21). *Malcolm X assassination: 50 years on, mystery still clouds details of the case.* The Guardian. Accessed December 1, 2020 from https://www.theguardian.com/us-news/2015/feb/21/malcolm-x-assassination-records-nypd-investigation

Justia. (1966). *United States of America, Appellee, v. Walter Augustus Bowe, Robert Steele Collier, and Khaleel Sultarn Sayyed, Defendants-appellants, 360 F.2d 1 (2d Cir. 1966).* Justia:US Law. Accessed December 1, 2020 from https://law.justia.com/cases/federal/appellate-courts/F2/360/1/390905/#fn1_ref

NYC, Department of Information Records. (n.d.). *Unlikely historians: Materials collected by NYPD surveillance teams, 1960-1975.* NYC Archives, Department of Information Records. Accessed December 1, 2020 from https://www.archives.nyc/unlikely-historians/intro

Rachell, L.E.J. (2019) *Incognegro: How Law Enforcement Spies on Black Radical Groups.* Columbian College of Arts & Sciences: History News Network. Accessed December 1, 2020 from https://historynewsnetwork.org/article/173226

Viola Jr., David C. (2017) *Terrorism and the Response to Terrorism in New York City During the Long Sixties.* Dissertation, City University of New York. Accessed December 1, 2020 from https://academicworks.cuny.edu/cgi/viewcontent.cgi?article=2955&context=gc_etds

Appendix

a. Raymond A. Wood's Confession Letter. Signed January 25, 2011. *(Document has been redacted for legal purposes.)*

1

January 25, 2011 TO WHOM IT MAY CONCERN

I Raymond A. Wood being of sound mind and body wish to confess the following:

I was a black New York City undercover police officer from April 1964 through May of 1971. I participated in actions that in hindsight were deplorable and detrimental to the advancement of my own black people. My actions on behalf of the New York City Police Department (BOSSI) were done under duress and fear that if I did not follow the orders of my handlers I could face detrimental consequences. Presently, I am aging with failing health; recently I have learned of the death of Mr. Thomas Johnson and are deeply concerned that with my death his family will not be able exonerate him after being wrongly convicted in the killing of Malcolm X.

The Facts are as follows:

April 17, 1964. I was hired by the New York City police department. Without training I was immediately assigned to the BOSSI investigation unit.

My job was to infiltrate civil rights organizations throughout New York City, to find evidence of criminal activity, so the FBI could discredit and arrest its leaders.

After witnessing repeated brutality at the hands of my coworkers (Police), I tried to resign, Instead I was threatened with arrest by pinning marijuana and alcohol trafficking charges on me if I did not follow through with the assignments.

Under the direction of my handlers I was told to encourage leaders and members of civil rights groups to commit felonious acts.

The Statue of liberty bombing idea was created by my supervisor/handler. Using surveillance the agency learned that Bowe and Sayyed were key players in Malcom X's crowd control security detail. It was my assignment to draw the two men into a felonious federal crime, so that they could be arrested by the FBI and kept away from managing Malcolm X's Audubon Ballroom door security on February 21, 1965. On February 16, 1965 The Statue of Liberty plot was carried out and the men were arrested just days before the assassination of Malcolm. At that time I was not aware that Malcolm X was the target.

On February 21, 1965 I was ordered to be at the Audubon Ballroom, where I was identified by witnesses while leaving the scene. Thomas Johnson was later arrested and wrongfully convicted to protect my cover and the secrets of the FBI and NYPD.

I have placed my full confession into the care of my cousin [redacted] I have requested that this information be held until after I have passed away.

It is my hope, that this information is received with the understanding that I have carried these secrets with a heavy heart and remorsefully regret my participation in this matter.

Raymond A. Wood

b. Brownmiller, Susan. (1965, Jun 3). "Statue of Liberty Case. View from the Inside: I Remember Ray Wood." The Village Voice, Pages 3 & 11

Susan Brownmiller is an accomplished feminist author, journalist, and activist. She gave her permission to include her article "Statue of Liberty Case. View from the Inside: I Remember Ray Wood." in this book

Page Three

WATCHES & CLOCKS

Statue of Liberty Case

View from the Inside: I Remember Ray Wood

by Susan Brownmiller

SIMMER

KAISER

ZEN

For the Cause

VID Collects For Greenville

THE WALLPAPER STORE

A wall system
should be designed with flair,
constructed with care,
look beautiful and be functional,
easy to assemble or disassemble,

View from the Inside: I Remember Ray Wood

Physical Metamorphosis

Entrained Again

Editorial Pictures

Prints Shown

Transcription:

Statue of Liberty Case

View from the Inside: I Remember Ray Wood

By Susan Brownmiller

"Ray Wood, let me tell you, I knew him, it was hysterical," screeched the pretty little redhead from the Village Independent Democrats. They had his picture in the papers the day after the arrests, the back of his head, and my husband said, "Honey, that's the guy we knew as Woodall." A few days later she unearthed some letters that the undercover police agent in the Statue of Liberty bomb plot case had written to her. Nice, chatty letters from a New York Negro involved in CORE to a pretty white acquaintance on a Mississippi summer project: "Dear Miss Blood and Guts," he wrote in an even hand, "Take care of yourself down there. Don't do anything rash…Mississippi is the whole United States of America…I'd like to take a rifle and go down and join you, but that's just daydreaming."

In one letter he enclosed some clippings of the summer's Harlem riots and offered his own eye-witness account: "I have seen cops beating cowering Negroes in the streets of Harlem." Was this confused and angry leftwinger Woodall talking or was this the cool and calculating policeman Wood establishing his identity as a cop-hating militant?

"Yeah, I knew him, like from around." The speaker was a Negro in his late thirties who left Harlem for West 4th Street many years ago. "What do you want to write about him for? He was just a guy who found a way to get ahead, that's all. You want to tear him down, just like you white liberals always try to tear a Negro down who's making it. He just found a way to make it a little, that's the Ray Wood story, so leave him be."

After the spectacular arrest of three New York Negroes and assorted white Canadians in the alleged Statue of Liberty bomb plot last February 16. U.S. Attorney General Nicholas Katzenbach fired off a letter to New York City Police Commissioner Michael Murphy with a note of special congratulations to Detective Raymond Wood for his "remarkable undercover work." To a covey of bewildered East Village chicks, "undercover" is an ironic sick joke. One determined young lady rang the old familiar number and was told by Wood-Woodall's roommate, "It's best if you don't call here again." Romance is chansey in the city of opportunity. Later, the number was disconnected.

For the Cause

In the middle of April of last year, shortly after the plans for the controversial World's Fair stall-in had been announced by three rebel New York City chapters of CORE, a tall, good-looking Negro wo called himself Ray Woodall walked into the Bronx CORE office and asked if he could work "for the cause." He dressed well, was soft spoken and said he was 27, a graduate of Manhattan College and currently studying law at Fordham. He indicated that this was his first militant civil-rights activity but mentioned a slight association with a Bronx reform democratic club with whom he was disenchanted because of their pussyfooting around on civil rights.``

If CORE had placed an advertisement in the Amsterdam News describing what it was looking for, Woodall would have fit the bill. For an organization which fought one wrenching battle against white domination and a second against black female leadership, Woodall was the prototype of the new Negro militant. "He was the all-American boy," said one Negro male associate. "He had such leadership ability, said a young white girl wistfully. Probationary membership requirements were winked at. Within two months Woodall was chummy with the executive board members of the

Bronx, Brooklyn, and Manhattan CORE chapters, and an elected delegate to CORE's national convention in Kansas City, where he chaired the dissident New York caucus. "In CORE we suspected the white folks as the cops of the organized leftists," says Dwayne Bey, a dedicated photography student and former activist from Brooklyn CORE, "but who would have looked at him."

This was a time of hectic organization and front-page publicity for CORE. Woodall sat-in at the World's Fair and slept-in at the Bronx Terminal Market construction site. He vigilled for Schwerner, Chaney, and Goodman at Foley Square and marshalled demonstrators at the Democratic convention in Atlantic City. During the Harlem riots he captained a picket line at police headquarters on Centre Street. When spirits were down, it was Woodall who led the group in freedom songs. He had a beautiful voice.

Ray Woodall was a man's man and a ladies' man. With the men he fooled around with Karate, smoked some and drank. He bartended at all the fund-raising parties. With the women, "Well it got so he couldn't go on a picket line because all the girls were chasing him," says a Village observer. "You know the expression. We call them "bagel babies." They go after anyone black in trousers. Woodall was cool. He was the sweetheart of the bagel set. Each girl thought she was the only one. I guess they just didn't want to see the truth.``

Physical Metamorphosis

Woodall was named Bronx CORE housing chairman and also put in charge of a voter registration project. "He goofed up," says a member. "We began to wonder if he was just jive talk and no action." An interesting physical metamorphosis occurred in Woodall as the summer progressed. The clean shirt and pants gave way to dirty blue denims. His hair grew longer.

The attempted citizen's arrest of Mayor Wagner was his last major activity with CORE. Woodall, Bronx CORE Chairman Herbert Callender, and a third participant were arrested when they stormed city hall to arrest the Mayor. Woodall, who had assiduously avoided arrest on other CORE projects, required special dispensation from the courts to prevent his being fingerprinted and thus possibly exposed. He apparently felt by this time that his work CORE was not as fruitful as he and his superiors had expected. He had found a few marijuana smokers among the fringe membership and witnessed illegal sale of drinks at the fund-raising parties at which he bartended. He had been able to tip off Centre Street to a couple of demonstrations before they occurred. CORE was getting disgusted with him, and he in turn said he was disgusted with them. He offered as proof of CORE's irresponsibility the fact that he had to pay his own (the police department's) money in court for the Wagner arrest.

During the summer of 1963, Raymond A. Wood, as off-and-on teletype operator, was genuinely studying a business course at Fordham (his third college try). He sent in a postcard to the Great Books club requesting information about their educational program, and Great Books sent a salesman, a serious young man named Paul Boutelle, to interview the prospective customer at his Bronx apartment. Boutelle and Wood hit it off nicely. They were both Negro, about the same age. Both were interested in self-improvement. They discussed Wood's finances and decided he couldn't possibly afford the $395 for the Great Books set. They liked each other well enough to exchange addresses and phone numbers, and before he left, Boutelle gave Wood some literature about a cause he was interested in, the Committee to Aid the Monroe Defendants. Neither man followed up the initial contact.

Untrained Agent

What Wood hadn't told Boutelle was that he had an application pending with the New York City Police Department. On April 18, 1964, Wood's appointment came through. On that day, and without preliminary training at the police academy, a highly unusual procedure, Wood was sent into CORE as an undercover agent.

In July of 1964, Boutelle, who had gotten immersed in politics as the chairman of the Metropolitan Freedom Now party, addressed a meeting at the Militant Labor Forum on University Place. Ray Woodall came over to him at the meeting's end, shook hands and said "Remember, you solicited me for the Great Books." Boutelle did remember the young man who had wanted to improve himself. He didn't think anything was strange about Wood becoming Woodall. "People sometimes shorten their names," he says. "I just made a new notation on the next page of my address book, marking down Woodall and his new Bronx address." Woodall told Boutelle he had been working with CORE but was disgusted with their hypocrisy.

By October of 1964, Woodall was working actively with Freedom Now, a group several degrees to the left of CORE. He told his new friends he had a job with Railway Express. Boutelle asked Woodall if he would like to be secretary-treasurer of Metropolitan Freedom Now, and Woodall agreed. Together they opened a checking account for the new party at a Chase Manhattan branch in the Bronx. They were the only ones empowered to sign checks. Boutelle believes, although he hasn't checked recently, that the account is still in existence, with a balance of $45.

Freedom Now had its organizational problems, but the two men became friendly. Boutelle introduced Woodall to Robert Collier, another friend of his who was working with Freedom Now. Walter Bowe, a Village jazz musician and judo instructor, fell by about that time, and so did Khaleel Sayyed. The young men palled around, attended YSA parties, showed each other Karate stunts, and tried to organize a series of lecture classes. Woodall was going to teach Negro history. Paul Boutelle had less time this fall and winter for politics. He was working for Great Books and driving a taxi cab at night. One day he read in the papers that Sayyed, Collier and Bowe had been arrested in a Statue of Liberty bomb plot, and that Ray Wood was a police agent.

Different Picture

The details or non-details of the bomb conspiracy will have their day in court. The conspiracy trial currently under way at the U.S. Courthouse on Foley Square, where Wood as Woodall had vigilled for the three from Mississippi, alternately pictures him as a hero cop or agent provocateur.

Roy Innis, a medical researcher at Montefiore Hospital and a leading member of Manhattan CORE, ran into Wood not long ago at a Chinese restaurant on upper Broadway. Wood was back in a clean suit and shirt. His hair was cropped. The two former friends were embarrassed at the chance encounter. "He told me he called some of the old people and they understood." In his recalls, "I gave him my new home phone number and told him to call me. I really wanted to talk to the guy. One thing I do understand. A policeman starts at $6000. How many Negroes out of high school or college can earn that? But he marched with us on picket lines and literally slept with us for days at a time on our demonstrations. He saw police brutality in Harlem. Didn't something of CORE have to rub off?''

Resource: the village VOICE, June 3, 1965

Made in the USA
Las Vegas, NV
03 March 2021